Advance Praise for Kathy Kelly's
Other Lands Have Dreams

"Activists have always battled the odds... It's a long haul. It's step by step. As Mahalia Jackson sang out, 'We're on our way'—not to Canaan Land, perhaps, but to the world as a better place than it has been before. It's what Kathy Kelly and her Voices in the Wilderness project is all about. She is a direct descendant of Dorothy Day, who when asked why she was making so much trouble for the authorities answered simply, 'I'm working toward a world in which it would be easier for people to behave decently.'"

Studs Terkel
author, *Hope Dies Last*

"*Other Lands Have Dreams* provides insight into the heart and mind of an extraordinary woman—known as 'Missiles' in a U.S. Federal prison and recognized as an American friend in the slums of Baghdad and Basra. Kathy Kelly shows her love of others and her commitment to nonviolence by standing courageously with the ordinary yet threatened people of America, Haiti and Iraq.

"She shows U.S. foreign policy to be what it is—ugly, violent, tragic and intrusive. She undermines this violence by her quiet inner peace and with her own presence in American prisons, in Haitian squalor and in Iraqi slums.

"She shares with readers the perception of a small Iraqi boy who unwittingly speaking for much of the world—after the events of 9/11—said he was feeling badly about the attack, but thought that Americans did not understand what happens to other people when they are hit by American bombs.

"Ms Kelly has a unique way of educating us by having us understand, almost experience the pain of others better. She has us look at ourselves, feel wanting, yet encouraged to do better and follow her relentless and non-violent lead."

Denis Halliday
former U.N. Humanitarian Coordinator for Iraq

"On reading these accounts of death and cruelty, we might well lose hope, but we are saved by the other stories, often less told, which Kathy records in her book. Stories of the courage and resilience of the ordinary Iraqi men, women and children, who continue to maintain their human dignity and in spite of everything yes, even in the midst of war, show kindness and hospitality to the strangers in their midst.

"These stories of Kathy Kelly's life and work, touch our soul and renew our hope and belief in humanity. They inspire and challenge us to work for justice."

Mairead Corrigan Maguire
Nobel Peace Laureate, 1976

Other Lands Have Dreams

From Baghdad to Pekin Prison

Kathy Kelly

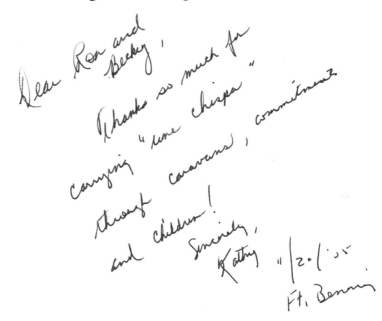

Dear Ron and
Becky!
Thanks so much for
carrying "una chispa"
through caravans, commitment
and children!
Sincerely,
Kathy 11/20/05
Ft. Benning

CounterPunch

Other Lands Have Dreams

From Baghdad to Pekin Prison

Kathy Kelly

CounterPunch
PETROLIA

AK
PRESS

FIRST PUBLISHED BY
CounterPunch and AK Press 2005
© CounterPunch 2005
All rights reserved

COUNTERPUNCH
PO Box 228 Petrolia, California, 95558

AK PRESS
674A 23rd St, Oakland, California 94612-1163
www.akpress.org

PO Box 12766, Edinburgh, Scotland EH89YE
www.akuk.com

ISBN 9781904859284
ISBN 1-904859-28-3
Library of Congress Control Number: 2005923965

A catalog record for this book is available from the
Library of Congress

TYPESET IN TYFA AND STAINLESS.
PRINTED AND BOUND IN CANADA.

DESIGN AND TYPOGRAPHY BY Tiffany Wardle
COVER ILLUSTRATION FROM "Bird of Paradise", 1992
(oil on canvas) by Suad Al-Attar. Private
Collection/Bridgeman Art Library International.

Contents

Milan Rai
Foreword
Kathy Kelly and The Long Wars

S TANDING WITH ORDINARY PEOPLE, WHETHER IN IRAQ OR IN U.S. jails, Kathy Kelly has challenged U.S. power, and challenged all of us to see the humanity and dignity of the victims of U.S. power. *Other Lands Have Dreams* is an inspirational book from someone who has made nonviolence into a compassionate confrontation, an active living force.

Nonviolence, which is active, which seeks to confront and change injustice, which does not shrink from the world, but which is a living force in the world, raises uncomfortable questions. Over thirty years ago, Noam Chomsky wrote of Daniel and Phil Berrigan that they had "a disturbing habit of posing hard questions, not only by what they write and say, but by what they do." Much the same could be said of Kathy Kelly, who has made her life a response to one of the hardest questions posed by the Berrigan brothers: are peacemakers prepared to take the same risks in making peace that soldiers are prepared to take in making war? Soldiers spend long periods separated from their families, in distant and unfamiliar places, enduring unpleasant conditions without much reward, risking themselves bodily and psychically, and, at the very least, facing the prospect of capture and detention for unforeseeable periods of life-time.

In various frameworks, some of which are referred to in these pages, Kathy Kelly and her companions have adopted these disciplines, which time and again have resulted in incarceration in jails and prisons. The challenge of making nonviolent social change, of making peace, has often included the challenge of enduring imprisonment. It could be argued that until many are able to face this challenge and this risk, our movements for peace will merely modify rather than force a halt to the making of war and the perpetuation of injustice. If this is so, the question of enduring prison becomes a strategic challenge for our movements. One way forward, illustrated in these pages, is to choose to see imprisonment as an opportunity to encounter other human beings and to celebrate them. This path is only open when fear is replaced by compassion and strength. Few have made this exchange as completely as the author of this book.

Throughout these grim and desperate years, Kathy Kelly has stood with the ordinary people of Iraq. She was in Iraq during the war of 1991 and during the war of 2003. Together with scores of volunteers from Voices in the Wilderness, she helped to bring out of Iraq stories of ordinary families faced with superpower brutality. She brought these stories out in the wilderness years of the late 1990s. She has brought them out again during the latest phase of occupation. Such stories have helped thousands to begin to understand the realities of our Iraq policy. They have helped to break the confines of state propaganda, particularly about the effect of sanctions forced via the U.N. on Iraq throughout the 1990s and up to 2003, at a terrible cost in Iraqi and particularly Iraqi children's lives. Mark the reach of this propaganda.

Sanctions and Propaganda

Just over a year after the invasion of Iraq, the prominent journal *Foreign Affairs* published a critique of President Bush's drive to war. George A. Lopez and David Cortright, academics involved in the Joan B. Kroc Institute for International Peace Studies at the University of Notre Dame, argued that the Bush Administration made a mistake in launching the invasion. Bush officials had failed to understand that U.S. policy towards Iraq was succeeding, not failing: "Washington discarded an effective system of containment and deterrence and, on the basis of faulty intelligence and wrong assumptions, launched a preventive war in its place."

Lopez and Cortright argued that: "The crisis of intelligence that pundits and politicians should be considering is not why so many officials overestimated what was wrong in Iraq; it is why they ignored so much readily available evidence of what was right about existing policies."[1]

The problem with the Bush Administration's approach to Iraq, according to Lopez and Cortright, was that it was not intellectually rigorous enough. Lopez and Cortright argue that before the 2003 invasion, U.S. intelligence agencies and policymakers "disregarded considerable evidence of the destruction and deterioration of Iraq's weapons programs," and "consistently ignored volumes of data about the impact of sanctions and inspections on Iraq's military strength." A misjudgment as to the current state of Iraq's military capabilities led to an unnecessary war.

As Lopez and Cortright claim in the title of their article, "Sanctions Worked." The authors argue that "despite Saddam's recalcitrance," the record now shows that U.N. inspections "decapitated Iraq's banned weapons programs and destroyed the infrastructure that would have allowed it to restart clandestine programs." They point out, correctly, that inspections were accepted by Baghdad only under duress from economic sanctions. They therefore conclude that inspections-backed-by-sanctions "worked."

In the real world, U.S. policy time and again subordinated both disarmament and inspections in Iraq to more important policy goals. In the real world, sanctions "worked" in that they made the economy and the people "scream," as President Nixon instructed in the case of Chile.[2]

Restricting our attention to the military aspect of these grim years, Cortright and Lopez fail to recognize that the disarmament process in Iraq had two dimensions: detection and destruction of weapons, on the one hand, and prevention and monitoring, on the other. The second aspect, referred to as "Ongoing Monitoring and Verification," involved the installation of cameras and other detectors throughout Iraq's scientific-industrial base to prevent the reconstruction of any WMD programs.

In 1998, the United States sabotaged the vital "Ongoing Monitoring and Verification" program—leaving the world blind in Iraq—first to pursue a coup attempt against Saddam Hussein, then to launch a military strike against Iraq.[3]

The Disarmament Disaster

During 1998, relations between Baghdad and the U.N. weapons inspectors (UNSCOM) reached a new low. Baghdad sought reassurance from the Security Council that verified disarmament would lead to significant changes in the sanctions regime. Article 22 of U.N. Security Council Resolution 687 said that once nuclear, chemical, biological and missile disarmament had been verified, the oil embargo on Iraq would be lifted. The U.S., with crucial British support, refused to reaffirm this vital paragraph during the autumn of 1998. Washington and London "rejected proposals by Russia, France and China that would have clearly committed the Security Council to a lifting of the oil embargo if Iraq complied with requirements to eliminate its weapons of mass destruction."[4] As a result, on October 30 1998, the Security Council wrote a letter of "clarification" to Baghdad which refused to reaffirm Article 22. This letter, reportedly "drafted by Britain," "triggered Saddam's decree on October 31 that stymied UNSCOM entirely." The London *Independent* commented, "Saddam had some reason for anger—the integrity of Article 22 is crucial for him."[5] The *Financial Times* reported that "Mr. Saddam's decision to cripple UNSCOM was triggered by the U.S. refusal explicitly to commit itself to lifting the oil embargo if Iraq complied with disarmament requirements—as stipulated by" Article 22 of U.N. Security Council Resolution 687.[6] *The Economist* observed, "Iraq interpreted this as confirmation of its long-held—and plausible—belief that, even if it did come clean on all its weapons, no American administration would lift the oil embargo so long as Mr. Hussein remained in power."[7]

In other words, far from using sanctions as part of a carrot-and-stick approach to gain Iraqi compliance with U.N. weapons inspections, as Lopez and Cortright assume, Britain and the United States refused to continue offering the inducements promised in a Security Council Resolution, and this led immediately and predictably to Iraq ending co-operation with the inspectors. Far from sanctions "supporting" the system of inspections, the sanctions were used—by Britain and the United States—to undermine the inspections.

Iraq's weapons were not the central concern. Inspections were not the central concern.

This was clearly demonstrated in the following weeks. In his memoirs, the head of the U.N. weapons inspectorate, Australian diplomat Richard Butler records that on December 15, 1998 he was invited to the office of the U.S. Ambassador to the U.N. Peter Burleigh. Burleigh advised the UNSCOM chief to be "prudent" regarding the safety and security of the U.N. weapons inspectors in Iraq. Butler writes, "I told him that I would act on this advice and remove my staff from Iraq."[8] UNSCOM inspectors were withdrawn from Iraq within hours, never to return. Shortly after their withdrawal, the U.S. bombed Iraq using information gleaned from the inspectors. It then became known that U.S. intelligence had planted spying devices throughout Iraq—inside equipment belonging to the U.N. weapons inspectors.[9] Former inspector Scott Ritter also aired his conviction that U.S. intelligence officers employed as inspectors inside Iraq had used their inspection activities to attempt to coordinate a coup against Saddam Hussein using elite Special Republican Guard officers.[10] After all these revelations Iraq refused to permit U.N. weapons inspectors to return to Iraq, and the discredited UNSCOM was scrapped.

UNSCOM chief Richard Butler, a faithful servant of U.S. policy, reflects in his memoirs, "If one uses the test of looking rationally at outcomes, without ascribing motives, it could be argued that the death of UNSCOM also became U.S. policy, because that is what has happened."[11]

In other words, Washington decided to put its own political-military objectives in Iraq ahead of weapons disarmament: by planting spying devices inside UNSCOM equipment; by using inspectors to mount covert operations inside Iraq aimed at decapitating the regime; and by ordering inspectors out of Iraq in order to carry out a massive bombing raid (Operation Desert Fox).

To repeat: Iraq's weapons were not the central concern. Inspections were not the central concern. The inspectors were ordered out of Iraq by Washington, not by Baghdad.

Returning to Lopez and Cortright, in their analysis the only criterion of success or failure is the impact of any measures on Iraq's WMD capacity. By this criterion, U.S. and British sanctions policy was a failure, because both the sanctions regime and the inspection agency were manipulated in such a way as to collapse the disarmament effort, and to bring to an end effective monitoring of Iraq's WMD capabilities. The only means of preventing the reconstruction of Iraq's WMD programs were destroyed as the foreseeable consequence of U.S. and British policy decisions.

Lopez and Cortright criticize U.S. Government policymakers for a lack of intellectual rigour, when their own analysis of the sanctions-and-inspections tragedy is far from rigorous. The Bush Administration's case for war and the Clinton Administration's case for economic sanctions were intellectually flawed, but it is the moral and legal failings in their policies towards Iraq that should be at the center of discussion, whether that discussion takes place in scholarly journals or in the public arena.

The Humanitarian Disaster

In an article of over 4,500 words entitled "Iraq Contained: Sanctions Worked," Lopez and Cortright devote just over 100 of those words to the humanitarian impact of the economic sanctions. In passing, they note that coupled with the damage caused by the Gulf

War bombing, sanctions "helped spur" a "severe humanitarian crisis" that resulted in "hundreds of thousands of preventable deaths among children during the 1990s." "For the first six years, comprehensive sanctions cut Iraq off from all world trade and shut down its oil exports, devastating its economy and society." This is referred to as "the initial humanitarian cost" of sanctions; after the inception of the U.N. humanitarian "oil-for-food" program in 1996, the "hardships" of Iraqi civilians apparently began to "ease."

The basic argument of the Lopez-Cortright critique was pronounced clearly by then U.S. ambassador to the U.N. (later U.S. Secretary of State) Madeleine Albright, in what may become the defining exchange of the Clinton era, when she was asked on May 12, 1996, by CBS presenter Lesley Stahl, "More than 500,000 Iraqi children are already dead as a direct result of the U.N. sanctions. Do you think the price is worth paying?" Albright responded, "It is a difficult question. But, yes, we think the price is worth it."[12]

Did sanctions work? Was the price worth it? These are questions that can only be answered affirmatively by people who have lost their moral compass.

The simple fact is that U.S. policy was not governed by the need to disarm Iraq in between the 1991 Gulf War and its successor in 2003 (disarmament was a desirable but not a primary goal). An examination of the termination of inspections in 1998 demonstrates that Washington had higher priorities than inspections and disarmament. Washington preferred sanctions-without-inspections to inspections-without-sanctions.[13]

If we turn our attention to the 2003 invasion, it is clear that once again U.S. policy was not governed by the need to disarm Iraq, and that once again Washington had higher priorities than inspections and disarmament. That is why Colin Powell, supposed dove among the hawks, said in January 2003: "The question isn't how much longer do you need for inspections to work. Inspections will not work."[14] Despite such assertions, significant disarmament took place in the following weeks. By March 7, 34 al-Samoud-2 missiles, including four training missiles, two combat warheads, one launcher and five engines were destroyed under U.N. supervision. Chief weapons inspector Hans Blix described this to the Security Council as "a substantial measure of disarmament – indeed, the first since the middle of the 1990s."[15] George W. Bush signaled his lack of interest in such disarmament by dismissing these events: "He [Saddam Hussein] will say words that sound encouraging. He's done it for 12 years. He has got a lot of other weapons to destroy, why hasn't he destroyed them yet?"[16] Iraqi disarmament was just "a last minute game of deception," something to be brushed aside on the road to war.[17]

In reality, disarmament was just a cover. The issue of weapons of mass destruction was just a pretext for maintaining sanctions and then prosecuting a full-scale war. The policy remained the same throughout the period from 1990 to 2003. The assault on Iraq in January 1991 did not end in February of that year, but merely shifted in mode. The long war continued via the most restrictive and crushing sanctions regime the world has ever seen, and then culminated in the explosion of violence in March 2003.

This is the dark saga and there have been no more courageous witness against its terrible toll than Kathy Kelly and her comrades in their group Voices in the Wilderness.

A brief chronology of U.N. economic sanctions against Iraq 1990-2000:

August 2, 1990	Iraq invades Kuwait
August 6, 1990	U.N. imposes comprehensive economic sanctions on Iraq (Security Council Resolution 660)
January 17, 1991	U.S.-led coalition launches war against Iraq
Feburary 28, 1991	Iraq withdraws; U.S.-led coalition ends war
April 3, 1991	U.N. continues comprehensive economic sanctions on Iraq (Security Council Resolution 687)
March 17, 1996	First Voices in the Wilderness sanctions-breaking delegation to Iraq
December, 1996	U.N. "oil-for-food" humanitarian program for Iraq begins
September 30, 1998	U.N. Humanitarian Coordinator for Iraq, Denis Halliday, resigns in protest at sanctions
August 12, 1999	UNICEF, the U.N. children's agency, estimates that 500,000 more children have died in Iraq since 1990 than would have died if the conditions of the 1980s had been maintained
February 14, 2000	U.N. Humanitarian Coordinator for Iraq, Hans von Sponeck, resigns in protest at sanctions

Notes to foreword

1   George A. Lopez and David Cortright, "Containing Iraq: Sanctions Worked," *Foreign Affairs*, July/August 2004. Available from http://www.foreignaffairs.org. A short cut to the article is available at http://tinyurl.com/4d4oc.
2   To see a photograph of the handwritten notes of the meeting in which Nixon gave this order, please go to http://www2.gwu.edu/~nsarchiv/NSAEBB/NSAEBB8/ch26-01.htm.
3   William Arkin, a U.S. military commentator, has suggested that the bombing raids were actually targeted at the regime's internal security apparatus, "using the intelligence gathered [secretly] through UNSCOM." William Arkin, *Washington Post*, January 17, 1999, cited in Sarah Graham-Brown, *Sanctioning Saddam: The Politics of Intervention in Iraq* (London, 1999), p. 103 n.
4   *Financial Times*, November 2, 1998.
5   *Independent*, November 13, 1998.
6   *Financial Times*, November 12, 1998.
7   *Economist*, November 7, 1998.
8   Richard Butler, *Saddam Defiant: The Threat of Weapons of Mass Destruction and the Crisis of Global Security* (London: Phoenix, 2000), p. 224.
9   This was revealed by Barton Gellman of the *Washington Post* in January 1999: "Annan Suspicious Of UNSCOM Role; U.N. Official Believes Evidence Shows Inspectors Helped U.S. Eavesdrop on Iraq," *Washington Post*, January 6, 1999, p. A01, cited in Dilip Hiro, *Neighbours not Friends: Iraq and Iran after the Gulf Wars* (London: Routledge, 2001), p. 118.
10 Scott Ritter, *Endgame: Solving the Iraq Problem Once and for All* (New York: Simon & Schuster, 1999), p. 144.
11 Richard Butler, *Saddam Defiant: The Threat of Weapons of Mass Destruction and the Crisis of Global Security* (London: Phoenix, 2000), p. 228.
12 Cited in Dilip Hiro, *Neighbours not Friends: Iraq and Iran after the Gulf Wars* (London: Routledge, 2001), p. 120.
13 The various resolutions of the Security Council offered the following sequence: if Iraq complied with inspections, oil export sanctions would be lifted, then inspections-monitoring would continue indefinitely to prevent the reconstruction of Iraq's WMD capabilities. Inspections would continue without sanctions.
14 *Independent*, 23 January 2003, p. 1.
15 Hans Blix, "Oral introduction of the 12th quarterly report of U.N.MOVIC," March 7, 2003 http://www.un.org/Depts/unmovic/SC7asdelivered.htm.
16 *Sunday Times*, February 23, 2003, p. 2.
17 *Daily Telegraph*, February 6, 2003, p. 1.

Milan Rai founded Voices in the Wilderness UK and has written several books: Chomsky's Politics, War Plan Iraq *and* Regime Unchanged.

Overture

HAD ONLY A FEW DAYS REMAINING IN MY JANUARY 2002 TRIP TO IRAQ.
I awkwardly asked if it would be possible to spend some time with
kids who weren't suffering from illness and poverty. The next day,
I was taken to the Baghdad School of Folk Music and Ballet. The children there were buoyant. Their school, one of the finest in the Middle
East, taught Arab and Western classical music, dance and art. I wandered in and out of classrooms, marveling at how obviously this
school "worked." In the art department, I happened upon a display of
children's drawings, one of which, done with pastel magic markers
and chalk, showed a jumbo jet plunging into the left hand tower of
the World Trade Center.

"Do you think I could meet the person who drew that picture?" I
asked the children. And then they were like their own little secret
service; in three minutes they had the artist there, all of eleven years
old, and he was so proud. I asked him, "Can you tell me what was on
your mind when you drew that?" He squared his shoulders, and he
said, "Allah wanted this to happen to people in America, so people in
America understand what happen to other people when America hit
them." By then his teacher had sidled up, and he saw her face, and
then he said, "and we love the people in America, and we want to be
their friends."

So I told him about being in New York City on September 11th. I
told him about families that had carried banners that said our grief is
not a cry for war, even though they themselves had lost loved ones.
And then I started to tell these kids about a song that had been sung
at one hundred fifty of the memorial services for people killed on
September 11th. I told them it was a peace anthem that celebrated the
common aspirations of people and what we experience in common
with one another, and they said, "Yes madam, and why you not teach
us this song?"

Well, I was in trouble, because my Arabic isn't that good and my
voice isn't much better, but the director of the school, Hisham al

Sharaf, had come and he doesn't understand the concept of not being able to do something. Within a day, he and a foreign ministry worker and our driver had gotten together and transliterated this song into Arabic and the kids were singing it to me, with the bargain that I would bring it to audiences in the United States as often as I could.

FROM: "THIS IS MY SONG" (O FINLANDIA)
LYRICS: LLOYD STONE: MELODY: JEAN SIBELIUS

This is my song, Oh God of all the nations,
A song of peace for lands afar and mine.
This is my home, the country where my heart is;
Here are my hopes, my dreams, my sacred shrine.
But other hearts in other lands are beating,
With hopes and dreams as true and high as mine.

Oh hear my song, oh God of all the nations,
A song of peace for their land and for mine.

It may sound contrived, but the fact is that the tape of school-children singing that song is the only item that survived looting and ransacking of the Baghdad School of Folk Music and Ballet after the U.S. Shock and Awe invasion of Iraq. Hisham al Sharaf came to me after the invasion had begun, after he'd tried my way to defend his school—talking, pleading with armed looters to leave it alone, or at least only to take valuables, not destroy the instruments and papers—and he had the tape in the palm of his hand. And I listened to it on a tape recorder with earphones, and I started to just sing along. Then I stopped because he was shedding tears.

Other lands have dreams. Please accept this book as testimony to the dreams of people in Iraq, people in prison. This book is dedicated to the children of Iraq.

Acknowledgements

Albert Camus concludes his essay, "Neither Victims nor Executioners" with this observation: "Over the expanse of five continents throughout the coming years an endless struggle is going to be pursued between violence and friendly persuasion, a struggle in which, granted, the former has a thousand times the chances of success than that of the latter. But I have always held that, if he who bases his hopes on human nature is a fool, he who gives up in the face of circumstances is a coward. And henceforth, the only honorable course will be to stake everything on a formidable gamble: that words are more powerful than munitions."

It's hard to imagine two people more committed to Camus's belief in the written word's power to combat war making than Alexander Cockburn and Jeffrey St. Clair, who've edited and published this book. Both work, intensely, to counter the structures and beliefs that underlie war. The thoughtful discourse enabled through Counterpunch is an indispensable resource for alternative media and education. I was frankly astonished that two people already so immersed in writing, speaking, and editing would undertake the challenge of helping me write.

Alexander Cockburn guided this book at every step and gave me the full benefit of his patience, humor and kindness. Jeffrey St. Clair, who originated the idea for this book, likewise extended his amazingly efficient helping hand and wise advice. I am glad and grateful!

Much of this book was written while I stayed in small hotels in Iraq and Jordan, or while I was imprisoned in U.S. Federal Correctional Institutes. I hope better times are ahead for all who've befriended me while living with them in those hotels and prisons. I'm particularly indebted to Sean Reynolds for faithfully helping me edit each article. To Ramzi Kysia and Ed Kinane, special thanks for helping me write from Iraq. To Sr. Cynthia Brinkman and Ruth Carter, more thanks for helping me write while in prison. Don Terry's thoughtful questions have been a great help in prompting needed reflection. Tai Little's and Alya Rea's proofreading skills were indispensable. I'm deeply indebted to all my companions in the Voices In The Wilderness campaign and especially to Jeff Leys and Laurie Hasbrook who ably coordinated our efforts while I was lost in the wilderness of this book.

For initially publishing many of these essays, I'm grateful to editors of *The Progressive, Hope, Fellowship* and of the following websites: www.counterpunch.org, www.commondreams.org, www.antiwar.com, www.electroniciraq.net, www.dissidentvoice.org. Abiding thanks to Scott Blackburn for ably maintaining the Voices In The Wilderness website: www.vitw.org. Thanks also to Josh Warren-White and his colleagues at AK Press. For the remarkable creativity that comes through listening, my deepest thanks to Studs Terkel. He can best be likened to a magnificent redwood tree.

PART ONE

Catching Courage

I GREW UP ON THE SOUTHWEST SIDE OF CHICAGO IN AN AREA SAUL Bellow described as "rows and rows of bungalows and scrawny little parks." I was the third of six children. It was a secure environment. I thought Mom, Dad, the parish nuns and priests, Officer Friendly, and the crossing guards were all part of a benign cabal to keep the Kelly kids happy.

My mom and dad met in London in 1944 during the Blitz. Dad was a GI with a desk job, a sergeant who had joined the army shortly after leaving the Christian Brothers religious order in which he'd spent half his life. Mom studied nursing at a place where the students cared for children with disabilities. Prior to that she'd been an indentured servant in Ireland, where she was born, and then in England.

My mom was set to marry a British Royal Air Force pilot, who was declared missing in action. Then she met and married my dad, gave birth to my older sister Pat, and bade farewell to Dad who was shipped back to the U.S. with a boatload of GIs. Then, as mom waited for the brides to be shipped out, the pilot turned up. "Katen, I'm home!" It's a wonder any of us were born. My mother wasn't very charmed by bleak Chicago.

I don't think my parents spoke much about the war when we were kids. My brothers and sisters and I have felt like investigators, trying to pull out the details. They spoke of heading into the subways when the sirens blasted, of feeling dismay when a building was hit which they knew had civilians in it.

My mother gave birth to three children in one year (the twins, Maureen and Mike, are eleven months apart from my brother Jerry). Eventually, Maureen's crib was moved into the room Loretta and I shared. Pat had a room to herself. When all of us were living under one roof and the babies had outgrown their cribs, I ended up on the living room couch for a "bedroom," but I don't remember that being much of a bother because I was in high school, working a part-time job in the Chicago Loop, and tired enough to fall asleep during *"The Tonight Show."*

Our neighborhood was a crucible for most of the social problems afflicting U.S. society in the fifties and sixties—racism, sexism, militarism, and classism. We wouldn't have heard those last three words used, but as the civil rights movement developed, the racism in my neighborhood was quite evident.

By the time I began studies at St. Paul-Kennedy High School, African Americans had moved into housing projects at Le Claire Courts on Cicero Avenue, and teenagers from families in that area had begun to attend Kennedy. My school was a "shared-time" experimental school where we attended a private Catholic school for part of the day and the local public school, one block away, for the other part. I remember expecting lunchroom riots at the public school. During my senior year, we sometimes had policemen, with dogs for hall guards. Glass bottles and ceramic plates had been removed from the cafeteria for safety. It wasn't unusual for the cafeteria to suddenly empty out into the fields outside because of lunchroom fighting between black and white students.

I remember walking past neighborhood mothers who stood on the corner outside our school shouting racial epithets at African Americans as they entered the building.

Once, during an afternoon class, white football players ran down the hall, some carrying others on their shoulders, screaming "Kill the N-----!" My teacher was working on a problem at the blackboard. She walked over to the hallway, closed the door, and finished the board work. No mention of a problem in the hallway. I had a lump in my throat and couldn't see the blackboard through my tears, but there was no way, at that point, that I would have raised my hand or my voice. I do remember a small group of us approaching the principal of the public high school to tell him that we were troubled, and I think certain teachers may have encouraged us to do so, but we were close to graduation. After the graduation turned into a near-riot scene, with racial slurs called out throughout the listing of graduates' names, I guess I was just glad to turn the page on that chapter.

At St. Paul High School, I was enamored with every one of my teachers and felt challenged and inspired by them. They were young nuns and brothers, mainly, along with a few lay teachers. The Rev. Dr. Martin Luther King Jr.'s teachings were compared to gospel passages; we were encouraged to become part of tutoring programs so that we could better understand people who were from different backgrounds than our own. We read about Dan Berrigan, a Jesuit priest who steadily resisted the Vietnam War and U.S. nuclear weapons buildup. Berrigan said that one of the reasons we don't have peace is that the peacemakers aren't prepared to make the same sacrifice demanded of the soldiers. I wondered what it would mean to give over one's whole life, or to risk one's life, for peacemaking.

The entire school gathered one day to watch the quasi-documentary, *Night and Fog*, made by Alain Resnais. The filmmaker showed the empty Nazi death camps after the survivors were liberated. With haunting classical music in the background, a narrator explained that nothing was wasted. The film showed piles of blankets made from human hair, lampshades and drawing paper made from human skin. The cameras focused in on an efficiently designed crematorium, then showed railroad tracks leading up to one of the death camps. Did the tracks cross through villages? Did nearby neighbors smell the burning flesh? At a deep emotional level, I never wanted to be a spectator, a bystander, sitting on my hands or standing on the sidelines in the face of unspeakable evil.

Maybe I romanticize the small private school, and certainly I could have done more to become involved in the larger, more institutional public school. But I'm still grateful for the adults at the small school having broken the code of fatalism that was part of my upbringing, a fatalism that stated it was okay to talk about a problem, okay to analyze it, but if you thought you could do something about it, you were "too big for your britches." The St. Paul faculty gently but consistently showed us hero figures who acted bravely to confront injustice and cruelty and who believed in love of enemy as well as love of neighbor. Some of us also listened to discussions between our parents and these young teachers. I felt glad that my parents respected the teachers. One way the teachers earned respect was through fostering personal relationships with people from the neighborhood.

Despite my desire never to sit on the sidelines, I managed to go through most of the Vietnam War like Brigadoon in the mist. It was easy to hate the war. But I never went to a demonstration, never called an elected official to express my antiwar sentiments, never passed out a flyer, or wrote to an imprisoned resister.

I did write a long paper about initial involvement of U.S. ground troops in Vietnam, after which a little "behavior mod" kicked in—the professor liked the paper, which motivated me to read news analysis about Vietnam.

Altruism isn't a word I'd ever have used then, but I think about it now. I wanted to be a helper, wanted to fit helping into a fairly madcap schedule. There are plenty of ways to be decent and helpful in this world without ever getting involved in politics, foreign affairs, or antiwar efforts. My former husband, Karl, once told me that he felt many people are a bit like woodchucks, burrowing their way into comfortable surroundings, harming no one, helping many, and that there's not a thing wrong with such a way of life, except that we live in a world where inordinate amounts of power are concentrated in the hands of a relatively small number of people whose visions and goals are deeply flawed. The metaphor helps me better understand why fine and even noble people sometimes seem disinclined to take a risk in confronting war.

Following another seminar on the Vietnam War, I attended a presentation by a representative of the Catholic Peace Fellowship, Tom Cornell, a prominent pacifist who protested the Vietnam War. He said that we could and should make a difference, that if we didn't try, who did we think would? I remember walking home, alone, and feeling a giddy sense of liberation. I found an elderly Jesuit who had visited the campus, Father Forsyth, SJ, and asked him more about the Jesuit Volunteer Corps that he'd recommended in a homily. (I had attended mass almost daily in 1974, my senior year.) He gave me application material for the JVC. I thought I'd like to go to Nome, Alaska. I was grabbing, happily, at straws. But that same week, my dad was first hospitalized for severe depression; it would have been a terrible time to leave Chicago.

Tom Cornell's literature included an order form for *Fellowship*, one of whose contributors was William Stringfellow. After reading a few of his articles, I looked for one of his books, *An Ethic for Christians and Other Strangers in an Alien Land*. Stringfellow was a lawyer and an Episcopal minister who had worked in Harlem. His scripture scholarship led directly to radical activism—no escape hatch! I remember reading Stringfellow while sitting under one of those horrible overhead hair dryers, baking my hair which was wrapped in orange-juice-can-sized rollers in one of thousands of efforts to straighten it out. Who knows? Maybe Stringfellow's stinging challenges to status quo America appealed to me because it offered a way out from under the nutty hair dryer! Anyway, the book sparked an intense desire to somehow become connected with those hero figures who were becoming more accessible by the time I was finishing a second year of graduate study.

Finally, during graduate studies at the Chicago Theological Seminary, I reached a point at which I simply couldn't continue writing papers about "the preferential option for the poor" and singing, at liturgies, "Our God Hears the Cry of the Poor." I'd been sending checks to the Francis of Assisi Catholic Worker House, a hospitality house in Chicago's impoverished Uptown neighborhood. One evening two "workers," Henry and Bob, came down to Hyde Park to check out Jimmy's Woodlawn Tap and decided to knock on my door first. I was out; they left a note encouraging me to visit the house, and about a month later I headed north with a friend who was a helper at the nearby soup kitchen. That was in the spring of 1977. I moved to Uptown that summer.

Forgive the cliché, but the grass never looked greener elsewhere. New friends in Uptown lived out the values that I'd been extolling in papers and exhorting in classrooms, and the collective determination to form a community that included street people, shut-ins, new immigrants, and whomsoever knocked on the door of the local Catholic Worker House was purely exhilarating and often tremendous fun.

Eventually Roy Bourgeois, a Maryknoll priest, moved into the neighborhood. His charisma led us to question why so many Central American refugees were fleeing their homelands. When Roy was locked up for six months after flinging blood on a poster of his friend, Rutilio Grande, who'd been murdered by U.S.-funded death squad members, it upped the ante for our own sense of responsibility.

Once, during a prayer service for Roy at my apartment, a dozen of us were crowded into a small living room when Karl Meyer, an activist who we revered, dropped in with a challenge to join him in an action protesting draft registration. It was my first arrest. As the police came to take us off to jail, I was trembling. Karl thought I was afraid—I was, but not of the police or jail. I was terrified of saying something stupid in front of him!

Karl and I were married for twelve years, and he is still my closest friend and mentor. He radicalized a generation of us who were part of the "do-gooders ghetto" in Uptown. He helped me understand that one of the greatest gifts in life is to find a few beliefs that you can declare with passion and then have the freedom to act on them. For me, those beliefs are quite simple: that nonviolence and pacifism can change the world, that the poor should be society's highest priority, that people should love their enemies, and that actions should follow conviction, regardless of inconvenience.

After several years of teaching religion and earning a Master's degree in Religious Education, I was hired to teach at St. Ignatius College Prep, a Jesuit institution and one of the top fifty schools in the country. Another faculty member, Al Schorsch, and I decided to become war tax refusers by lowering our salaries beneath the taxable income. I was earning $12,000 and officials at the school would distribute the $9,000 difference to other programs. I knew that I didn't want to pay for weapons. And I wasn't keen on the CIA, the FBI, the prison systems, U.S. intervention in Central America, and the almost complete failure of any governmental system to serve needy neighbors, many of them desperate, in Uptown.

One of the most important "spiritual directors" in my life has been the Internal Revenue Service. Janis Joplin's lyric, "Freedom's just another word for nothing left to lose," comes to mind. War tax refusers learn ways to become impervious to collection, and that generally means finding ways to live without owning property, relying on savings, or growing attached to a job that one couldn't leave in the event of an IRS notice about wage garnishment.

Becoming a war tax refuser was one of the simplest decisions I've ever made and one of the easiest decisions to maintain. I can't imagine ever changing my mind.

In the summer of 1985, the Jesuits gave me a professional development grant that enabled me to visit Nicaragua. The day after my arrival, close friends who were Maryknoll associates invited me to a gathering at the home of Miguel D'Escoto, the Foreign Minister who was part of the Maryknoll religious order. D'Escoto spent much of the evening outlining his plan to begin a lengthy fast "for peace, in defense of life, and against contra violence." He spoke at length about the cross, emphasizing that we must be willing to accept change and death. Then he talked about his confidence in the potential of Christians to make a difference, emphasizing that new ways and means must be tried. He spoke gently about nonviolence, his long, deep admiration for Rev. Dr. Martin Luther King, Jr., and his clear belief that Christians must be ready to bet their lives on their beliefs. He said he hoped to initiate new methods of resistance for people who were understandably war weary. He called his offering a *chispa*, a spark to ignite prayer and fasting throughout Nicaragua. D'Escoto especially hoped that in response to this prayer and fasting Christian communities worldwide would work to end U.S. military support for the contras.

The next day, I traveled to San Juan de Limay, in the north of Nicaragua. Children there were radiant and friendly, many of them too young to understand that during the previous week U.S.-funded contras had kidnapped and murdered twenty-five people in their village. Later that summer, I joined the fast with Miguel D'Escoto and listened to stories pour forth as many hundreds of Nicaraguan peasant pilgrims gathered with him, eager to show solidarity with the priest-minister's desire to nonviolently resist contra terrorism. D'Escoto urged those of us from the U.S. to return to our homes and develop nonviolent actions there commensurate with the crimes being committed.

In 1986, in mid-semester I resigned from my job as a teacher at St. Ignatius College Prep. In a letter to the students and faculty, I wrote: "As many of you know, I spent seven weeks in Nicaragua this summer.... As a result of all that I have seen and heard, I have reached a strong conviction that the United States is doing a terrible and evil thing in financing the contra attacks against Nicaragua." I explained that I was quitting my job to devote myself full time to opposing contra aid and that I found it intolerable to be comfortably at liberty in a country where people will stand by or accede to crimes against the life of another people. I knew that being part of the nonviolent protests which Karl and I were planning would mean quitting my job and being prepared for arrest.

Don Terry, a reporter for *The Chicago Tribune*, once pressed me to list every time I've been arrested. "I don't know," I wrote to him. "When I'm in a jail cell by myself I sometimes try to remember past experiences and I nearly always fall asleep after the first dozen or so.

- five times with Karl protesting draft registration,

- twice begging Senator Percy to investigate Roy Bourgeois' disappearance in El Salvador,

- five or six times for posting pictures of victims on the Federal Building walls during the contra attacks, about a dozen or more sit-ins and die-ins at the Federal Building while more money poured into the coffers of Central American dictators, mercenaries, death squads,

- five times for planting corn on nuclear missile silos,

- at least five times for protesting at Project ELF, five times for bringing lentils and rice to the steps of the U.S. Mission to the U.N.,

- three other protests, same site,

- twice for protests at the U.S.S Intrepid docked in NYC's harbor, once for sitting in at the Israeli consulate,

- once for sitting in at the French consulate (nuclear weapons testing in Tahiti),

- once at SOA, once for piping up after Madeleine Albright's acceptance speech when she was appointed Secretary of State,

- once for interrupting her talk at the Chicago Council on Foreign Relations,

- once for knocking every ten minutes on the office doors of Northwestern University's development planners just to let them know that an Iraqi child died once every ten minutes and encourage them to reconsider inviting Ms. Albright to give a commencement address (the address was canceled, we were also fasting for 12 days),

- once with Karl for handing out fliers at a military base in Florida protesting Clinton's 1993 bombing of Iraq,

- once for blocking troops planning to leave a national guard base for duty in Honduras,

- once for climbing a wall at a PSYOPS facility in Arlington Heights,

- three times for singing alternative Christmas carols at Water Tower Place ("We Three Crooks of contra-gate, lie and steal and manipulate, what was covert became overt, head for the shredding machine.....Oh, Ohhhh, shred the documents, shred the tapes, shred the proof and leave no trace. Fawn will help us, Casey will die for us, Reagan will just forget."),

- five times for entering federal judges' courtrooms and refusing to leave until they met with us about the U.S. violation of international law in bombing Nicaragua's Puerto Corinto,

- once for refusing to sit down, before a judge, while holding up pictures of Central American victims when we were finally launching a motion after getting a case in court, once for contempt of court for refusing to do community service under the auspices of that judge and challenging him to do his community service and hear the case, once for failing to show up for a trial in Florida (the time Karl and I leafleted in front of the PX at the military base, ...works like a charm, I'm dozing off!).

Don also asked me about arrests in other countries.

- the Israeli occupied West Bank,

- twice (Jericho and Ramallah); I've been flung around a bit by Israeli soldiers and intentionally "just missed" by their bullets,

- a Croatian military commander detained six companions and me for several hours, threatening us with deportation, but eventually let us go,

- likewise, a Haitian military commander detained several Christian Peacemaker Team companions and me for several hours, but then released us with orders to never hand out literature or speak in public about political issues. We then began a silent fast, sitting on a park bench in the town plaza. If someone approached us we'd put a finger to our lips and shake our heads. Everyone knew exactly why we were there. One old woman came up to us and did a quick little dance, threw back her head and laughed. "Yes, I know," she said, "some demons are only cast out by prayer and fasting,"

- Italian police detained us at Aviano, in the summer of '93, outside the U.S. Air Force Base there, for trying to chain ourselves to the fence, but they let us go. We fasted for the next seven days, urging the U.S. pilots not to fly bombing missions over former Yugoslavia.

I returned to teaching in the fall of 1987, working at Prologue High School, an alternative school for youngsters in my own neighborhood. Prospective students had to prove that no place else would allow them to enroll. The students, numbering about fifty, were members of rival gangs. At the end of each year, we planned more funerals than graduations, since at least three young people would have been killed by drive-by shootings and other gang violence. When my colleagues told me that Shawn Powell, a student who was exceptionally bright but plagued by traumas of growing up in a dreadfully troubled home, had been shot dead, I knew that I couldn't continue my work without taking a stronger stand against policies that allotted billions of dollars toward weapons buildup while young people in blighted urban areas could barely survive their teen years.

For the next twelve months, I joined activists from Chicago, Milwaukee, Madison and Kansas City to plan "Missouri Peace Planting." We were determined to plant corn on many of the 150 nuclear missile silos that surrounded Kansas City, Missouri, as a way to demonstrate that land was meant to grow corn and wheat and never to harbor weapons of mass destruction. That summer, before heading to Kansas City, I would bike out to abandoned industrial lots in Chicago to practice scaling fences. I'm not very limber and couldn't bear the thought of being caught on the barbed wire atop a missile silo's fenced enclosure. On August 15, 1988, fourteen of us carried out the action at various missile silo sites, simultaneously. I planted five kernels of bright pink corn at the missile silo, just what I could fit in my pocket, and hung two banners, "Disarm and Live," and, "You Can't Hug A Child With Nuclear Arms."

After hanging the banners, I sat on the cement lid over the nuclear weapon. Mist was rising from the ground, birds were chirping, crickets creaking. Then I heard a vehicle in the distance, racing along the country road. Arriving in a cloud of dust, three soldiers clambered out of a U.S. military jeep with a machine gun mounted on top. The soldiers wore camouflage, with helmets, combat boots, and walkie-talkies. They surrounded the perimeter of the site and crouched down. One said into his walkie-talkie: "All personnel please clear the site." I would do anything they said, at that point, as we weren't at all sure how they might react. (Our presence might not have been a surprise—we'd notified Whiteman Air Force base, in west-central Missouri, that we would engage in nonviolent civil disobedience at nuclear missile silo sites at some point over the summer.) "Raise your arms. Step to the left. Step to the right." They opened the gate, instructed me to walk out of the site, handcuffed me and then told me to kneel down. Two of the soldiers took off in the military vehicle—maybe they needed to check a manual to see what came next (as this was new for all of us)—leaving one soldier, standing behind me, with his gun aimed at my back.

After a short while, I began talking to him, looking straight ahead. I told him a bit about what motivated my friends and me to do this. I told him about students I'd taught at Prologue High School. I talked about homeless and hungry people in my own neighborhood and cited some statistics about the cost of nuclear weapons. I said that we were concerned for children and families in the Soviet Union as well, and that we hoped our actions would help children in his family too. Then I asked him if he thought the corn would grow.

"I don't know, ma'am," he said, "but I sure hope so." When I asked him if he'd like to say a prayer, he said, "Yes, ma'am." So I recited the Peace Prayer of St. Francis, "Lord, make me a means of your peace, where there is hatred let me sow love, where there is injury, pardon, ...sadness, joy ...grant that I may not seek so much to be consoled as to console, to be understood as to understand, to be loved as to love, for it is in giving that we receive, it is in pardoning that we are pardoned, it is in dying that we are born to eternal life."

"Amen."

And then: "Ma'am, would you like a drink of water?"

"Oh, yes, please, thank you."

"Ma'am, would you tip your head back?"

I wish I'd turned around so that I could see what happened next. Was there a flask attached to his belt? I don't know—I just know that he poured water into my mouth. He must have used both hands to give me that drink of water. We didn't disarm the nuclear missile silo sites of Missouri that morning, but one soldier took a risk and put down his gun to perform an act of kindness for a perfect stranger.

I was sentenced to a year in prison for planting corn on nuclear missile silos. I emerged from prison with an even greater resolve to remain faithful to Miguel D'Escoto's *chispa*.

In 1990, as it seemed increasingly likely that the U.S. would declare war on Iraq following Iraq's invasion of Kuwait, I volunteered to join the Gulf Peace Team, an international encampment of peacemakers on the Iraq side of the Iraq-Saudi border. "You can't be a vegetarian between meals," quipped Amman Hennacy, a co-founder of the Catholic Worker movement. "And you can't be a pacifist between wars."

I went there as a convinced pacifist, wanting to express a vigorous opposition to the war. We were at the border for the first fourteen days of the air war, and then Iraqi officials evacuated us to the Al Rashid hotel in Baghdad. Four days later, after a bomb struck a lot adjacent to the hotel, Iraqi authorities again evacuated us—this time to Amman, Jordan.

I stayed there for six months. When I returned to the U.S., most people seemed to have forgotten about Operation Desert Shield. I returned to teaching and, during vacations, participated in several more peace team efforts. In the summer of 1993, after I returned from a peace team effort in Croatian controlled Bosnia, my dad moved into my apartment and I became a full-time caregiver for him.

I loved my father very much, but initially I was dismayed over what seemed a likely end to my involvement in peace teams, as I could barely manage a part-time teaching job and still be available for my dad. As it turned out, however, our small apartment eventually became "headquarters" for an unusual international experiment in peacemaking.

By 1995, several of us realized that the Gulf War over which we'd been willing to risk our lives had never ended. It had changed into a kind of war that is more devastating, more brutal than even bombardment. Reports were emerging from Iraq that showed that hundreds of thousands of children under age five had died during the most comprehensive state of siege ever imposed in modern history.

In December, 1995, several people who had been in Iraq before, during, and after the first Gulf War met at my apartment in Chicago to devise a nonviolent challenge to the U.N./U.S. economic sanctions. Calling ourselves "Voices in the Wilderness," we issued a letter to U.S. Attorney General Janet Reno on January 15, 1996, declaring that we would break the sanctions as often as possible by bringing medical relief supplies and medicines to children and families in Iraq. We were informed by the U.S. Treasury Department that if we continued with our plan we would risk 12 years in prison and a one million dollar fine. We thanked the Treasury Department for the clarity of their warning, asserted that we would be governed by the law of love, and invited U.S. officials to join us. That was the beginning of a campaign that sent seventy delegations to Iraq. I traveled there twenty-six times.

Voices in the Wilderness has always been "headquartered" in the three-bedroom apartment where I live. Caregiving for Dad became a natural part of Voices work as volunteers came to live at "Voices" and help develop the campaign. My Dad felt great affection for these activists. Typically, any volunteer's first stop after entering our door was at Dad's bedside to say a good word, hold his hand, and see if he needed anything. Appreciative bonds grew between Voices workers and my siblings. We sometimes joke, when asked how Voices was funded, that we embezzled from my Dad's Social Security check. But no one doubted, least of all my Dad, that the last years of his life were marked by unexpected and very welcome friendships.

My father died in May 2000. We never quite sold him on the idea of pacifists going to war zones, but at the end of his life he was convinced that wars should be abolished. I feel stubborn in my own belief that, although we would need to become many more than we are now, the efforts to send unarmed peace activists into zones of conflict are an arrow pointing to a viable alternative to war-making.

Consider, for instance, the small Christian Peacemaker Team which I joined in the summer of 1995, in Haiti. Had our team, which lived in a small town in the southern finger of Haiti, been copied one hundred times over, throughout Haiti, I think the violence being wreaked on Haitian people could have been diminished. I was only there for three months, but others who were there for a longer stay recorded the Haitian commandant saying: "I am ashamed and embarrassed that it was left to the foreigners on the hill to preserve the peace and security of this region." And how did we do that, we foreign women? We had Birkenstock shoes, spiral notepads, pens, and sleeping bags. Every morning we woke up and walked as far as we could and took notes from anyone who wanted to tell us of fears, anxieties, abuses that they were nervous about or that had actually happened. As it turned out, the militia folks in that area who had been threatening their neighbors didn't want to be on our list.

Every week we would use a ham radio to get those messages back to the United States, and from there send it via e-mail across the entire network of Christian Peacemaker Team people who were primed to act on these reports. It's significant to me that the funding for that team was almost nil. And though the Haitians did welcome the U.S. military when it came, our way would have worked if there had been enough of us to make a larger difference.

I've seen peace teams make mistakes. I've been a part of making many of those mistakes. I can arrange them topically, geographically, chronologically, so you and I can learn from them. I think we must continually explore the potential for going into situations of violent conflict, going in massively, going in before the deterioration is so great that people are ready to kill and torture and punish the ones who at one point have been their neighbors. How would resources ever become available to help create teams of people who could accomplish this massive intervention? Could we cut just one percent of our military budget and put it directly into creating such teams of people ready to go into situations of conflict to bring peace?

One of the greatest disappointments in my life is that we were unable to be a *chispa*, a spark that would ignite a nationwide demand to end the suffering of Iraqi civilians under the economic sanctions. Seventy Voices in the Wilderness delegations traveled to Iraq and returned with the images and stories of ordinary Iraqis, most of them children, bearing the brunt of punishment under economic sanctions. Those sanctions didn't cause Saddam Hussein to miss a meal— why didn't our efforts to break the economic sanctions and to return with "embargoed" stories of what we had seen and heard ignite "actions commensurate to the crimes being committed?"

When pictures emerged from Abu Ghraib prison in 2004, showing the torture inflicted on Iraqi detainees, those images became iconically embedded in people's consciences around the world and within the United States. Had we been able to present to U.S. people the conditions endured by vulnerable and innocent people in Iraq, especially children, under the economic sanctions, I don't believe those sanctions would have withstood the light of day.

• • •

DURING THE 1980S, I LOOKED FORWARD TO ANNUAL VISITS FROM TWO heroes of mine, Ernest Bromley and Maurice McCracken. They would stop in Chicago en route to nonviolent direct actions planned by the Jonah House community in Washington, D.C. Because these two veterans of civil rights struggles, antiwar movements and numerous disarmament actions practiced near total non-cooperation with arresting authorities, they were heading into difficult straits each time they joined in the Jonah House events. At times they were treated brutally by police officers. Mac had been dragged by his hair and prodded with an electric stun gun. Ernest nearly died when he refused food and water in a Washington, D.C. lockup. I remember shyly asking Ernest, soon after I'd first met him, "Don't you ever feel afraid?" "Oh, now, don't let anyone ever tell you they don't feel fear," said Ernest, folding his arms and crossing his long legs. "Everybody feels fear," he said. "Courage is the ability to control your fear." "Ernie's right," Mac added. "And, you see, we catch courage from one another."

In the days just before the Shock and Awe bombardment began, Iraqi friends at the Al Fanar Hotel, in Baghdad, shook their heads and smiled when I told them that a hardware store in my Chicago neighborhood had run out of duct tape, plywood and plastic as people, panicked by supposed threats to U.S. security, rushed to reinforce their windows in advance of a U.S. attack against Iraq. My neighbors in Chicago had been consumers of an astonishing marketing campaign, designed to sell the U.S. war against Iraq. They were convinced that Iraq posed an imminent threat to their safety. As early as September 2002, publicists for the Bush administration began "selling" the war. They knew how to manipulate and hyperinflate people's fears.

In Baghdad, shortly before the war, even I and fellow Iraq Peace Team members were deeply disconcerted as we huddled around a short-wave radio, on the balcony of the Al Fanar hotel, listening to Secretary of State Colin Powell detail twenty-nine instances of "evidence," supposedly uncovered by U.S. intelligence, that Saddam

Hussein's regime possessed weapons of mass destruction. We had believed the reports of chief U.N. weapons inspector Hans Blix and former weapons inspector Scott Ritter, both of whom stated that the tasks of disarming Iraq were near completion. It seemed then that U.S. intelligence had sufficient proof to undermine those claims. Now, the U.S. weapons inspection teams have left Iraq, and none of the weapons of mass destruction we were told to fear have been found.

Ernest and Mac's advice is more timely than ever. What if U.S. public opinion hadn't been so vulnerable to fears which prompted majority approval for the war? What if the U.S. public hadn't allowed such fears to suppress valid questions and cautions? Suppose the vast majority of the U.S. public had rejected the possibility of isolating our country as a nation to be feared for following a "go it alone" policy based on threat and force. Suppose public opinion had clamored for linkage with allies who wanted to seek nonviolent means to further disarm Iraq. What if U.S. media had steadily covered the scandal of using economic sanctions to target Iraq's most vulnerable people— the poor, the sick, the elderly, and the children?

Courage is the ability to control your fear and courage is contagious. I'd add to those definitions an additional truism that can help dissolve fear: treat other people right, and you won't have to be afraid of them.

Each Voices in the Wilderness delegation treated people in Iraq with respect and warmth. Overwhelmingly, Iraqis we met responded with hospitality, friendship, generosity, and unfailing good will, in spite of the fact that we hailed from countries, the U.S. and the U.K., which insisted on maintaining the sanctions against them. Even when the U.S. repeatedly bombed innocent civilians in the so-called "no fly" zones, we returned from trips to Iraq unable to answer the question "why do they hate us so much?" and instead wondering "why do they love us so much?"

But how long can you expect people to keep extending a hand of friendship when, in return, they're pummeled by siege, bombardment, and an abusive occupation?

During the U.S. bombing in March and April of 2003, I saw how children suffer when nations decide to put their resources into weapons and warfare rather than meeting human needs. All of us at the Al Fanar hotel learned to adopt a poker face, hoping not to frighten the children, whenever there were ear-splitting blasts and gut-wrenching thuds. During every day and night of the bombing, I would hold little Miladhah and Zainab in my arms. That's how I learned of their fear: they were grinding their teeth, morning, noon, and night. They were far more fortunate than the children who were survivors of direct hits, children whose brothers and sisters and parents were maimed and killed.

Now, as occupying forces, coalition soldiers are understandably fearful when they face a population wearied and angered by the relentless suffering they've endured. The best way forward would be to find the courage to admit that the U.S. made a colossal mistake. And then to look for ways to rectify the situation by showing Iraqis that the U.S. is willing to close its bases, issue timetables for troop withdrawal, assist with clean-up in Iraq of depleted uranium, cluster bombs, landmines and other unexploded weapons, and pay restitution to Iraqis who suffered loss as a result of the past 14 years of economic and military warfare waged by the U.S.

Reconstruction of Iraq should be funded by the U.S. and its allies, but directed by and for the benefit of Iraqi citizens. Iraqis should be employed to rebuild Iraq and paid a living wage. Finally, the U.S. should renounce any effort to create, in Iraq, a puppet government with strings attached to the U.S. national interest. In 2004, the U.S. spent 67 billion dollars on force protection and maintenance for the U.S. military while allocating 20 billion dollars for reconstruction. Suppose those sums were reversed and a priority had been placed on giving jobs to Iraqi companies as the main recipients of assistance for reconstruction. That would have been a step in the direction of treating Iraqi people fairly. If they had reason to trust us, we might have less reason to fear being there.

My friends, Ernest and Mac, died within two weeks of each other, in the winter of 1997. We can still catch courage from them, and from the many people who stood shoulder to shoulder with them, clamoring for civil rights and human rights. But to catch on to their brand of courage, we'll need to slow down and use that time to think about the truly frightful relations the U.S. has created with other countries whose resources we want to control and exploit. Coming to grips with the unsustainability of our economic and social patterns is difficult. Most of us probably feel a real fear of changing our lifestyles in ways that allow us to live more simply, consuming less and wasting less.

We can catch courage from one another to make those changes. By doing so, we can feel heartened, not threatened, by the simple truth that most of the time, if you treat people right, you don't have to be afraid of them.

The stories that follow tell about interactions between very ordinary people, from Iraq and the U.S., who caught courage from one another during a time of war.

PART TWO
Letters from Iraq

OR SEVEN YEARS, VOICES IN THE WILDERNESS MEMBERS TRAVELED TO Iraq with a pittance of medical relief, earnestly wanting to offer some kind of hope, but mainly able only to whisper, "We're sorry. We're so very sorry," as we sat, helpless, at bedsides of agonized children.

Even those words caught in my throat in April, 1999 at the Dijla Secondary School for Girls in Baghdad. "They are really angry," the headmistress apologized, eyebrows raised. Leila, age sixteen, rose soon after we entered the class. A voice that should have been bursting with life and excitement, at her age, was high-pitched, fraught, anxious. "You come and you say 'You will do. You will do,'" said Leila, pleading and accusing at once. "But nothing changes! All what we see is paper, promises. Me, I am sixteen. Can you tell me what is the difference between me and someone who is sixteen in your country?"

Sitting next to her, Fatima, also sixteen, recounted horrific memories of the Gulf War, then described a more recent visit to relatives in a village north of Iraq during the 1998 Desert Fox bombing. "Why?" she asked. "Tell us. What have we done? Can you imagine if Iraq did this to another country?" And then Nasra: "My father directs the electric company here. But I study by kerosene lamp at home. And this is to name only one human right. Most tragic, we watch children die. We are helpless! Who are the criminals?"

In the first years of our travel to Iraq with Voices in the Wilderness delegations, we urged reporters to visit hospitals and witness for themselves the abject suffering of patients desperately needing medicines and equipment unobtainable under economic sanctions. "Now it's different," I wrote, in the late spring of 1999. "One needn't even leave the hotel lobby." I had just witnessed an encounter between Jeff Guntzel, one of our delegation members, and Mehdeh, a hotel worker in his early twenties. Mehdeh seldom sought anything for himself and exuded a quiet, dignified manner. That day, he grabbed

Jeff's arm, seemingly panicked. "Please, Mister Jeff," he pleaded, "last night our family was together in one room, in the dark, there was no electricity. And we lit the kerosene lamp. Someone got up to use the bathroom and the lamp turned over. My sister, she is twenty, she is going to be married in two months, but now three quarters of her body is covered with burns, and her eyes. To pay for the surgeon, we need 60 dollars more. Please, Mr. Jeff, can you help us?" The poison of these sanctions touched almost every home.

And still, it seemed that no amount of pain or sorrow would cancel or interrupt the hospitality extended toward us.

In February 1998, I traveled to Iraq with a British Voices in the Wilderness team. The U.S. was threatening another massive bombardment. We decided to go to Fallujah in hopes of better understanding the perspective of people whose marketplace had been bombed in 1991 by a British smart bomb that went astray. The blast instantly killed 150 people and wounded hundreds. By the time of our visit, many more had suffered and died during nearly eight years of brutally punitive economic sanctions. At Fallujah's main market, we began distributing a leaflet about why we were violating the economic sanctions. Throngs of people pressed toward each of us, eager for leaflets. Separated from my companions and surrounded by people shouting at me as they grabbed leaflets, I began to wonder if this could turn into an ugly scene. One man who spoke English stood in front of me, his eyes blazing. "You Americans! You Europeans!" he shouted. "You come to my home. I show you water you not even give your animals to drink and this is all what we have. And now you want again to kill our children. You cannot kill my son. My son, he was killed in al harb Bush (the first Bush war)." Suddenly he stopped. Looking at me closely, he said, "Ah, Madame, you're too tired. You come with me, take something to eat." He steered me through the throng to a small falafel stand and brought me a cup of tea. Then he urged me to find the rest of my teammates and bring them to his home for lunch.

In 1999, I returned to the Fallujah marketplace, this time with our friend Ahmed, a U.S. citizen, born in Sinai, who translated for us as we encountered a very similar scene. I spotted a child staring at me. He seemed about eleven years of age, quite poor, intense. "Ahmed, please," I asked, "ask this young man what he is thinking." The young boy squared his shoulders and said, "I am a scholar of the faith." Ahmed posed my question again. This time the answer was direct. "Tell her that I am thinking about how I will become a fighter pilot when I grow up," said the boy, whose gaze never swerved from mine, "so that I can bomb the United States."

Then Ahmed said, "Kathy, look, pay attention to this man," pointing to an elderly, balding fellow with huge jowls and white whiskers who had observed my encounter with the youngster. Large tears rolled down his cheeks. We were suddenly forlorn.

It was natural to weep. Yet no Iraqi child could afford our pessimism or cynicism. We were resolved to end the cruel and dangerous economic warfare against Iraq, to refute the notion that sanctions were necessary to combat the Iraqi regime and thereby enhance everyone else's safety. In fact, the economic sanctions had strengthened Iraqi President Saddam Hussein. We anticipated that if Saddam Hussein's authoritarian regime was replaced by a power vacuum, violent power grabs and uprisings could erupt, coupled with extreme vulnerability to incursions by neighboring states.

Beleaguered Iraqis assuredly didn't want to face added woes of civil war or invasion. Some Westerners who favored economic sanctions against Iraq suggested that the sanctions would force the Iraqi people to insist on a regime change. That seemed naive and unrealistic to us. If we truly wanted to help another country move toward positive social change, we would strengthen their educational institutions, assist them to develop effective social services, and improve their means to communicate both within their society and beyond.

Economic sanctions wrecked these same resources at every level. Schools and universities could barely function. The majority of Iraqis, desperately seeking to meet their most basic human needs, had little energy or time for any other endeavors. They searched for ways to put food on the table, cope with health problems, and handle emergencies. As for communication, one could ask any Iraqi student how it felt to be cut off from the revolutions happening as most societies adjusted to cyberspace. "We are trapped," said one bright graduate student in Baghdad, speaking of their enforced ignorance of the Internet. "We're in a dungeon."

I think often of Albert Camus' essay, "Neither Victims nor Executioners," in which he urges people never to be accomplices to murder. Maintenance of economic sanctions against Iraq required people in the U.S. to inflict child sacrifice, to aid and abet the most egregious instance of child abuse in the modern world. "And what have we done?" asked the young women I met at the Dijla school. "Who are the criminals?"

Nativity Under Siege
November 1998

First, the setting. In a particularly desolate area of Basra, Iraq's second largest city and a formerly thriving oil port, our van pulls up to a block of eight cement tri-level buildings, each a stark refuge for families who are "internally displaced."

Children dressed in rags scamper barefoot across oozing mud mixed with raw sewage. "Hello! Hello!" they cry out, surrounding us, grabbing our hands and pulling us toward their homes. They shout, "Surah!" the Arabic word for picture. Julie has pulled out her camera and they are eager to be photographed. Several children sidle up very close to me, and whisper, "Monies, Madame, monies." I feel myself sliding in a pile of slime and realize, as the children laugh with delight, that I've misstepped. My shoes are now caked with gooey mire. Anxious not to trek this filth into anyone's home, I duck around a corner, trying to separate from the crowd. Five youngsters join me, still beckoning me to come to their home, and when I point to my shoes, they shake their heads and laugh. They're right. The sewage and slime are pervasive, inescapable—befouling the water, the ground, the homes. Little tykes who disappeared into a nearby dark doorway emerge moments later with two young mothers, each carrying an infant. The mothers smile shyly, letting me admire their babies. We all pose for group photos.

The children's excitement and glee is irresistible, their innocence overwhelming. Have they any idea, I wonder, what dangers surround them? One open cut, one infection, one parasite could turn any one of the kids beaming up at me into a casualty of biological and economic warfare. Economic sanctions now claim the lives of five thousand to six thousand children every month. We're posing for pictures in a battleground.

Walking back to our van, we meet a little boy pulling a milk crate by a frayed rope. Inside the crate, bundled in a muddied, ragged blanket, a baby gazes calmly at us, undisturbed by the flies that rest on his face and lips. I notice his hair is reddish, a telltale sign of malnourishment. A bevy of children smile tenderly at the youngest among them.

In the coming month, many people in the U.S. and the U.K. will recall nativity scenes celebrating the birth and infancy of the child Jesus. They'd be horrified at the notion of a cruise missile exploding over the crèche. Most don't know that a modern-day Herod, deadly, vengeful, and reckless, pursues the little ones of Basra, waging biological and economic warfare, while threatening bombing strikes.

Each Sunday in the Christian season of Advent, churchgoers anticipate the arrival of the innocent one, born into utmost poverty, who will bring forth justice for the poor, liberty for captives, sight for the blind. "O come, O come, Emmanuel," is sung in churches worldwide. I hear the tune now and feel haunted. Is it possible, is there some dim chance, that good-hearted care could extend to the Iraqis in Basra?

When I left the U.S. a week ago, individuals and groups around the world were urgently responding to cries for help from victims of Hurricane Mitch. A week ago, it was okay to care about Nicaragua's and Honduras's children. This week, or next week, might it finally be acceptable to care about Iraq's children? Instead of perverting the U.N. into an instrument of warfare that brutalizes and kills children, might the potential to care for innocents in distress displace the missiles, sanctions, and media-hyped hatred aimed at Iraq? This Christmas, could a new birth of compassion and love arrive on time for Basra's children?

Banning Child Sacrifice: A Difficult Choice?
March 9, 1998

On February 9, our small delegation of two from the U.K. and six from the U.S., representing thousands of supporters, traveled to Iraq carrying 110,000 dollars' worth of medicines. We were the eleventh Voices in the Wilderness delegation to deliberately violate the sanctions as part of a nonviolent campaign to end the U.S.-led U.N. economic warfare against Iraq.

From previous trips, we knew exactly where to find overwhelming evidence of a weapon of mass destruction. Inspectors have only to enter the wards of any hospital in Iraq to see that the sanctions themselves are a lethal weapon, destroying the lives of Iraq's most vulnerable people. In children's wards, tiny victims writhe in pain, on bloodstained mats, bereft of anesthetics and antibiotics. Thousands of children, poisoned by contaminated water, die from dysentery, cholera, and diarrhea. Others succumb to respiratory infections that become fatal full-body infections. Five thousand children under age five perish each month. Nine hundred sixty thousand children who are severely malnourished will bear lifelong consequences of stunted growth, brain deficiencies, and disablement. At the hands of

U.N./U.S. policy makers, childhood in Iraq has, for tens of thousands, become a living hell.

Repeatedly, the U.S. media describes Iraq's plight as "hardship." Video footage and still photographs show professors selling their rare books. Teenage students skip school to hawk jewelry in the market. These are sad stories, but they distract us from the major crisis in Iraq today, the story still shrouded in secrecy. This story is about more than just "hardship." This is the story of extreme cruelty, a story of medicines being withheld from dying children. It is a story of child abuse, of child sacrifice, and it merits day-to-day coverage.

A Reuters TV crew accompanied our delegation to Al Mansour children's hospital. On the general ward the day before, I had met a mother crouching over an infant, named Zayna. The child was so emaciated by nutritional marasmus that, at seven months of age, her frail body seemed comparable to that of a seven-month-old fetus. We felt awkward about returning with a TV crew, but the camera person, a kindly man, was clearly moved by all that he'd seen in the previous wards. He made eye contact with the mother. No words were spoken, yet she gestured to me to sit on a chair next to the bed, then wrapped Zayna in a worn, damp, and stained covering. Gently, she raised the dying child and put her in my arms. Was the mother trying to say, as she nodded to me, that if the world could witness what had been done to tiny Zayna, she might not die in vain? Inwardly crumpling, I turned to the camera, stammering, "This child, denied food and denied medicine, is the embargo's victim."

I felt ashamed of my own health and well-being, ashamed to be so comfortably adjusted to the privileged life of a culture that, however blindly, practices child sacrifice. Many of us westerners can live well and continue "having it all" if we only agree to avert our gaze, to look the other way, to politely not notice that in order to maintain our over-consumptive lifestyles, our political leaders tolerate child sacrifice. "It's a difficult choice to make," said Madeleine Albright when she was asked about the fact that more children had died in Iraq than in Hiroshima and Nagasaki combined, "but," she continued, "we think the price is worth it." Iraqi oil must be kept off the markets, at all costs, even if sanctions cost the lives of hundreds of thousands of children.

The cameraman moved on. "I'm sorry, Zayna, "I whispered helplessly to the mother and child. "I'm so sorry."

Camera crews accompanied us to hospitals in Baghdad, Basra, and Fallujah. They filmed the horrid conditions inside grim wards. They filmed a cardiac surgeon near tears telling how it feels to decide which of three patients will get the one available ampoule of heart medicine. "Yesterday," said Dr. Faisal, a cardiac surgeon at the Fallujah General Hospital, "I shouted at my nurse. I said, 'I told you to give that ampoule to this patient. The other two will have to die.'"

Associated Press, Reuters, and other news companies' footage from these hospital visits was broadcast in the Netherlands, in Britain, in Spain, and in France. But people in the U.S. never glimpsed those hospital wards.

I asked a cameraman from a major U.S. news network why he came to the entrance of a hospital to film us but opted not to enter the hospital. "Please," I begged, "we didn't ask you to film us as talking heads. The story is inside the hospital." He shrugged. "Both sides use the children suffering," he explained, "and we've already done hospitals." I might have added that they'd already "done" F-16's lifting off of runways, they'd "done" white U.N. vehicles driving off to inspect possible weapon sites, they'd "done" innumerable commercials for U.S. weapon displays.

While the U.S. plays political games, children are dying, and we have seen them die. If people across the U.S. could see what we've seen, if they witnessed, daily, the crisis of child sacrifice and child slaughter, we believe hearts would be touched. Sanctions could not withstand the light of day.

I felt sad and shattered as we left Iraq. A peaceful resolution to the weapons inspection crisis was reached, at least temporarily, but Iraqi friends were intensely skeptical. "They are going to hit us. This is sure," said Samir, a young computer engineer. "Anyway, look what happens to us every day." Feeling helpless to notify anyone, we had left the scene of an ongoing crime.

Upon our return to the U.S., customs agents turned my passport over to the State Department, perhaps as evidence that, according to U.S. law, I've committed a criminal act by traveling to Iraq. I know that our efforts to be voices in the wilderness aren't criminal. We're governed by compassion, not by laws that pitilessly murder innocent children. What's more, Iraqi children might benefit if we could bring their story into a courtroom, before a jury of our peers.

Although we may be tempted to feel pessimistic, Iraq's children can ill afford our despair. They need us to build on last month's resistance to military strikes. During the Gulf War, I wasn't in the U.S. (I was with the Gulf Peace Team, camped on the border between Saudi Arabia and Iraq and later evacuated to Baghdad). I didn't witness, firsthand, the war fever and war hysteria. But when I returned to the U.S. people told me that the war had often seemed like a sporting event. Some people went to bars, raised mugs of beer, and cheered when "smart bombs" exploded on their targets. "Rock Iraq! Slam Saddam! Say Hello to Allah!" they shouted.

Last month, on February 18, 1998, college students shouted a vastly different cry. They didn't cheer the bombers, and in Columbus, Ohio, they may well have prevented deadly bombing missions. "One, two, three, four, we don't want your racist war." The lines confronted Ms. Albright, crackled across Baghdad. People on the streets smiled at me, an obvious westerner, and counted, "One, two, three, four..."

A week later, U.N. Secretary General Kofi Annan, at the conclusion of his remarks introducing a peaceful resolution to the weapons inspection crisis, (somewhat hypocritically, given the U.N.'s complicity in sanctions) urged young people around the world to recognize that we are all part of one another, to see the world not from the narrow perspective of their own locales but rather from a clear awareness of our fundamental interdependence. What a contrast between his vision of a new generation that wants to share this planet's resources and serve one another's best interests, globally, and the vision that Ms. Albright offers: "If we have to use force, it is because we are America. We are the indispensable nation. We stand tall. We see further into the future."

Ms. Albright's reference to "use of force" is the stuff of nightmares, given the ominous comments some U.S. military officials have made about preparedness to use even nuclear force.

I doubt that other nations will accept that the U.S. "stands tall." It's more likely that international consensus will conclude that the U.S. lacks the moral standing to be prosecutor, judge, and jury in a dispute over Iraq's policies. Most people in the Arab world believe that the U.S. favors Israel and is unwilling to criticize its actions, even when Israel violates international agreements or U.N. resolutions. People throughout the world point to the hypocrisy of the U.S. government in other aspects of international relations. The U.S. is over $1 billion in arrears in payments to the United Nations; it has ignored judgments by the World Court and overwhelming votes in the U.N. General Assembly whenever they conflict with its desires; and despite its rhetoric about human rights, the U.S. record of support for ruthless regimes is shameful.

Is it outlandish to think that courage, wisdom, and love could shape the formation of foreign and domestic policies? Is it overly optimistic to think that we could choose to ban the sale of weapons of mass destruction? Is it too much to ask that economic sanctions against Iraq be lifted and never again used as a form of child sacrifice? For the sake of all children, everywhere, let's continue sounding a wake up call to U.S. officials. They must stop punishing and murdering Iraqi children. The agreement negotiated by U.N. Secretary General Kofi Annan offers a basis for continued weapons inspections and the earliest possible end to the deadly embargo of trade with Iraq. The deeds of one leader, or even of an entire government, cannot be used to justify an unprecedented violation of human rights. Most Iraqis whom we meet hold no grudge against the U.S. people. It's time that we respond with remorse and regret for the suffering we've caused and with a commitment to end this racist war.

What About the Incubators?
April 5, 2000

It feels oddly like being at a wake in a funeral home. Our delegation members whisper together somberly as we wait to tour the Al Mansour Children's wing at the Saddam City Medical Center. The director is away, so someone has been sent to find a senior doctor to brief us. As I flip open my diary, it dawns on me that at this time four years ago, March 1996, the first Voices in the Wilderness delegation visited Iraq. Thirty delegations later, not much has changed within this hospital. What must the doctors and nurses think as one delegation after another hears the litany of shortages and views the dying the children?

When a doctor finally enters the office, my grim mood lifts immediately; it's Dr. Qusay Al Rahim, whom I've spoken of so often to so many groups in the U.S. My companions, meeting him for the first time, will probably feel the same warmth toward him as I do. He evokes a sense that we're working together to solve intractable problems, that even little gains, in the face of ridiculous odds, are rewarding. I wonder how he maintains his quiet, indomitable strength.

Two years ago, when I first met him, he solicitously accompanied us up to his ward, apologizing for the elevator that didn't work, the hallways that were dark because they had no light bulbs. Suddenly he raced away in response to a furor down the hall. Hospital visitors were shouting for help at the bedside of Ferial, a seven-month-old baby, whose mother was sobbing frantically. Ferial had just suffered a cardiac arrest. Dr. Qusay swiftly bent over her and administered mouth-to-mouth resuscitation. Ferial's heart gave out in a fight against malnourishment plus septicemia, a full body infection. The hospital lacked both the nutrients and the antibiotics this little one desperately needed. I watched Dr. Qusay face the anguished mother to pronounce the verdict, "I am sorry, but your child cannot live. We have not the oxygen, we have not the tube." How many times since then has Dr. Qusay felt shattered, having to speak tragic words to disbelieving parents?

Now he is explaining to us that in a very real way he thinks we are all fathers and mothers to these children, that it's a challenge to invent new ways to help them. And when something works, "Well, you see, this keeps you hopeful." He carefully details some of the greatest problems they presently face—they've run out of high protein biscuits formerly supplied by UNICEF, and they lack immunizations for MMR (measles, mumps, and rubella). Actually, batches of the vaccine do arrive, but electrical outages interfere with proper storage, damaging the medicines.

So far, his tone has been that of a kindly teacher who wants us to understand. But then he lowers his head and shakes it back and forth several times. "We had a terrible tragedy recently. Our incubators are old and broken down, but some we try to repair. We placed an infant inside a patched incubator, thinking it would work, but the sealant was faulty, and the baby grew very cold. In fact, we lost that baby."

I jot down in my notebook, "Incubators—mom!!" Shortly before the Gulf War began, I applied to join the Gulf Peace Team, a non-violent, non-aligned encampment that would position itself on the Iraq side of the Iraq-Saudi border, between the warring parties. The organizers placed me on a waiting list. In early January, 1991, I learned that I could join a U.S. contingent leaving on a plane that would be the last to land in Baghdad before the bombing began. Probably the most courageous thing I did during that year was to visit the Kelly home and tell my mother what I was about to do. She was vehemently opposed. Upon leaving, I caught a blast of frigid air in my face and my mother's thick Irish brogue at my back. "What about the incubators," she cried out, "Kathy, what about the incubators!"

She was referring to testimony from Nayirah, a young Kuwaiti girl, who told the U.S. Congress that she had witnessed invading Iraqi soldiers barge into a Kuwaiti hospital and steal the equipment. With luminous eyes and a compelling presence, she told of her horror as she watched the menacing soldiers dump babies out of incubators. Months later, when the war was a distant memory, reporters learned that "Nayirah" was actually the daughter of the Kuwaiti ambassador to the U.S., that doctors in Kuwait could not corroborate her testimony, that in fact the supposedly stolen incubators had been placed carefully in storage during the invasion, and that the Hill and Knowlton Public Relations firm had rehearsed with the young woman how to give apparently false testimony effectively.

Here are some things that are true.

The Desert Storm bombardment destroyed Iraq's electrical grid. Refrigeration units, sewage and sanitation facilities, and all sorts of valuable equipment were ruined. Life-saving devices found in a modern hospital were rendered useless. As the Allied bombing went on and on, my mother's question became more and more relevant, yet went largely unasked. "What about the incubators?"

Now, when our teams visit Iraq after nine and one half years of deliberate siege, we see incubators, broken and irreparable, stacked up against the walls of hospital obstetrics wards. Sanctions have prevented Iraqis from importing new incubators and from getting needed spare parts to repair old ones. And this is only one vitally needed item that sanctions prohibit.

Dr. Qusay's heroism is commendable. Earnest as ever, he tells us of other methods he wants to pursue, in the wake of the tragedy incurred by an irreparable incubator. "I have heard about, maybe you know it, the kangaroo method and this they do in Australia. I tell the mothers of tiny infants to try it. They can place the baby between their breasts and wrap themselves in a garment and this may keep the baby warm enough. Or I tell them to try to find gauze and cellophane and with this they might recreate conditions like an incubator. You see, we must invent and try to cope."

I wonder what would happen if Dr. Qusay testified before Congress as Nayirah did ten years ago. Would we respond with the same moral outrage now that such actions are American policy? Would we mobilize to end sanctions with the same fervor that drove us to destroy Iraq, and its incubators and its babies? Now as then, any mother, whether Kuwaiti or Iraqi, can tell you that child sacrifice is evil.

Healing Hands
January 8, 2002

In 1996, Dr. Raad Towalha gave up his career as a surgeon to become the director of Ibn Sina hospital in Mosul. Looking at his handsome and dignified figure, I quickly jot "could double for Omar Sharif" in my notepad. Like its director, Ibn Sina looks pretty good. Walking into the Cardiac Care Unit, I was surprised to see at least some machinery hooked up and blinking.

Then the litany: there are fourteen beds in the unit, but only two monitors, and there is no central control station. Who gets the two monitors? "I have no other choice," says Dr. Hamid Zacharia, the chief resident on the CCU. "I choose the most critical." In the event of an emergency, they rotate the equipment—it sounds like a bizarre game of musical chairs—removing the monitor from the patient formerly deemed most critical and hooking it up to serve the newly arrived patient.

An electrocardiogram machine was delivered, but alas, no paper.

They have a kidney dialysis unit, but lack filters.

Since 1996, when our first delegation visited hospitals in Iraq, we've heard the wretched litany of N/A—Not Available—over and over as frustrated doctors cite the missing items without which they can't heal their patients.

Dr. Zacharia has never been able to work in a fully equipped unit. His education has been inferior because of what he terms "scientific sanctions;" lacking textbooks and journals, he has learned much of what he knows about cardiac care through oral tradition. Older doctors describe what a "real" cardiac care unit would be like. Now he passes on this knowledge to younger resident doctors.

U.S. State Department officials have repeatedly told us that Iraqi doctors lack necessary equipment and medicines because the government of Iraq refuses to order sufficient quantities of needed goods and fails to distribute those that do arrive. Yet last week we heard a different account from Dr. Ghulam Popal, director of the U.N. World Health Organization in Iraq. He emphasized that WHO monitors are very satisfied with Iraq's distribution of needed items. Dr. Popal showed us a recent study indicating that 85 to 87 per cent of goods that arrive in the country reach the "end user" destination. The remaining 13 to 15 per cent of goods are held up in Iraq for purposes of quality control and for storage as buffer stock in the event of a national emergency (both policies recommended by WHO).

He also showed us the list of items needed for health care that have recently been placed on hold through the U.N. Sanctions Committee. Even out of the approved contracts, from Phase 1 of the Oil-for-Food program, which began in 1997, to Phase 10 which ended in 2001, only 57 per cent of approved items have reached Iraq. Some contracts that were approved in Phase 2 are just entering the country today, after a three-year delay.

"Under these conditions," says Dr. Popal, "you must expect shortages."

But Dr. Towalha and Dr. Zacharia believe that their biggest problems are emotional and psychological. Both are frightened and uncertain of the future. "If we lose the patient, we continuously blame ourselves," says Dr. Zacharia. "Yet, we need 'weapons' to fight disease. We are soldiers on the front lines without weapons."

They both express feelings of helplessness and frustration. "We rebuild our country. It is very difficult to see it attacked again. But if they plan to attack us again, what can we do?"

Dr. Towalha speaks of his personal future as a doctor. "We lose a generation of doctors. They become out of date. In two years, if you are not in contact with the outside, you are out of date." He points to himself, and says quietly, "One of them is me."

Dr. Towalha's hands are covered with thick, scaly scabs—the most severe case of psoriasis that I have ever seen. His condition forced him to stop practicing surgery. He mentions he also has a duodenal ulcer. Looking at his red and raw hands, he tells us that the methyltrexate needed to cure his condition is in short supply and very expensive. He shrugs slightly, "Stress can be a major cause of this disease."

Back in his office, he orders a round of tea. Our conversation eventually leads to his past. Since 1982, Dr. Towalha's younger brother, also a doctor, has been missing in Iran. He was last heard from on March 20, 1982.

"I lost two brothers, one in Iran; the other, my twin, during the Gulf War. This brother, my twin, has two daughters and one son." Dr. Towalha's eyes well up with tears and he quickly excuses himself. We make our goodbyes and quietly leave the hospital.

En route to Mosul, I'd read a report from the Washington Institute for Near East Policy, an American-Israeli think tank, about usage of psychological weapons to wear down the morale of Iraq's people. In it, Michael Eisenstadt, the report's author, writes, "Such efforts could keep Saddam on the defensive and create an atmosphere of crisis and tension." I wonder if Mr. Eisenstadt knows that more than one person lives in Iraq, and if he would regard Dr. Towalha's hands as a battle trophy? Do this kind doctor's feelings of guilt, anxiety, frustration, fear, helplessness, humiliation, uncertainty, and a penetrating, overwhelming sense of loss signal victorious gains for U.S. strategists?

Unfortunately, that answer is not available.

The Long Wait
January 12, 2002

In my fourteenth visit to Iraq, I came to know a little boy.

Five-year-old Munthedar, whose name means "waiting for," suffered from leukemia and thalessemia, and had just had his spleen removed when I first met him in early December, 2001. He barely noticed me. On my second visit he was sitting up and smiling, and by my third his mother said he'd been asking after me every day. He greeted me with kisses and shyly whispered, "Is there a toy for me?" Fortunately, I had one last toy harmonica to give to him. There aren't words to describe his mother's eyes as Munthedar clutched his tiny piece of plastic and flashed the gentlest smile I've ever seen. When I returned for a fourth visit, little Munthedar's bed was empty. He died Saturday, January 5, 2002.

Doctors and mothers in Baghdad hospital wards had taught us not to display grief and strong emotion in front of other children. It could frighten them.

Later, listening to the Baghdad Symphony rehearse, as the lights dimmed, I found a chance to express remorse. I wondered tearfully about the five-year-old whose joy over a plastic harmonica might have led to a life in music had he lived. Dreams, hopes, and lives snuffed out by a raging and vengeful embargo.

Month after month, the bullying went on, unchecked. The abuser hid in the muddle of hypocritical policies that no one involved really believed in.

U.N. officials, NGO coordinators, diplomats and U.S. State Department officials were painfully aware of the violence visited upon innocents in Iraq as a result of policies deemed genocidal by two U.N. humanitarian coordinators, Denis Halliday and Hans von Sponeck, who resigned their posts rather than cooperate.

To what could we liken U.N. acquiescence to murderously punitive policies that afflicted innocents? The U.N.'s relationship to the U.S. was that of a battered woman to an abusive partner, desperately going to great lengths to provide cover for her abuser. Battered women often struggle to gain some control over their situation by "cooperating" with the violence done to them—providing excuses and emotional support to their attacker.

When the U.N. Security Council, urged by the United States, approved the Oil-for-Food program, one U.N. official remarked: "We break their legs, then give them crutches." Another official expressed fear that confronting the U.S. too aggressively would undermine his agency's ability to pressure the U.S. to release some needed items, many of them medical items, from the list of goods on hold. When it was needed most, those officials were afraid to speak out. Instead, the U.N. quietly issued internal "Holds Bulletins," which tracked the holds placed by the U.S.—treating the stranglehold on Iraq as some sort of natural phenomenon, somehow out of anyone's control.

Battered women sometimes give up hope of entirely stopping their attacker, and simply try to control the extent of the beatings. Where hope lives, it is often in the lie that love comes at the end of a fist, and that if we only find the right sequence of words and caresses, the long wait for compassion can finally end.

But what's the message? Keep Daddy happy. It's my fault. Scream quietly, so the neighbors won't hear. And never let on that Daddy is vicious, selfish, dangerous, and absolutely out of control. The entire facade of bureaucratic delays that made up the U.N.'s efforts in Iraq was absurd. Did any of the U.N. workers who struggled to provide minute documentation that Iraq wasn't building bombs out of parts for water treatment plants, for example, really believe that the U.S. cared about their work? After five years of the Oil-for-Food program, it was clear that the U.S. was simply interested in finding excuses to maintain sanctions. Despite repeated denials, and incredibly detailed levels of "monitoring" and documentation by U.N. officials across every agency working in Iraq, the U.S. continued to pretend that Iraq was actively stockpiling food and medicine in warehouses and refusing to distribute it.

What could we have said to Tun Myat, the former humanitarian coordinator for Iraq, who at one point boasted to his staff that he was able to convince the Sanctions Committee to release some holds on equipment needed to repair Iraq's bombed out and dilapidated electrical grid? Over $4 billion in other desperately needed items, representing over 25 per cent of the entire Oil-for-Food program in Iraq, remained on hold.

I think of Munthedar, denied the therapy he needed, as he waited to die. What therapy could be prescribed for the U.N.?

We must resurrect the dream that created the U.N. out of the nightmare of WW II. We must show courage, wisdom, and love by acting now to confront a bullying, rogue superpower which refuses to allow the U.N. to act in accord with its own charter as world events bring all of us closer to the threat of expanded warfare and nuclear annihilation.

U.N. officials are responsible, now, to provide curative, ethical action and to stop postponing moral actions to some never reached future moment.

The alarm has sounded. It blares agonizingly in our ears, beckoning conscientious action. Tiny Munthedar sounded that alarm with faint breaths into a plastic harmonica, as he waited to die for the crime of being born Iraqi.

Siege Talk
January 22, 2000

"They know we own their country. We own their airspace....We dictate the way they live and talk. And that's what's great about America right now. It's a good thing, especially when there is a lot of oil out there we need."—Air Force Brigadier General William Looney, head of the U.S. Central Command's Airborne Expeditionary Force, which directs operations keeping Saddam Hussein's troops from flying south of the 32nd parallel.

The above quotation prefaced a recent edition of *Eat the State!*, an anarchist publication from Seattle. We wonder, does General Looney's blunt arrogance at least offer us some further insight into a basic dictate that the U.S. and Britain have for the people of Iraq? Distilled from recent State Department remarks and a PR saturation campaign surrounding passage of Resolution 1284, the message reads something like this:

"It's fine for the U.N. to call for a weapons-free zone, but we'll ensure that the only steps implemented toward achieving that goal are those that ensure that only Iraq is to be a weapons-free zone. We have no intention of stopping weapons sales to our allies in the region. We will have you surrounded with weapons of mass destruction, but you will have none. We'll be happy to take your oil, but we will have final control over how the revenue from your oil is spent. This is your punishment for having invaded Kuwait, despite the fact that it was only recently part of Iraq."

Iraqis hear this message from two countries, the U.S. and the U.K., which, for hundreds of years, have repeatedly invaded countries all over the world that were never part of their territory.

If the Iraqi government agrees to U.N. Resolution 1284, they must envision becoming subject to long-term domination by the U.S. and Britain, which can use their voting powers in the U.N. Security Council to form an economic and military protectorate over the government of Iraq.

If the Iraqi government yields to military domination, it will be allowed to have sanctions lifted, but it's clear that they'll have to yield the way Japan and Germany did after WWII, completely relinquishing sovereignty in the military domain.

Small wonder that the government of Iraq, still an independent country, rejects that neocolonial formula for domination. Quite likely, the U.S. and Britain designed Resolution 1284 anticipating that Iraq would never accept it.

Who or what can jar General Looney and others from believing that since the U.S. is the world's sole superpower, any ultimatum it issues must be accepted?

Ironically, Ms. Albright herself offers words of wisdom regarding what happens when, as a means toward an end, innocents are killed. But once again, she speaks with an overbearing arrogance that seems to occasion ethical blindness. Here are her remarks to leaders of the American Muslim community, December 21,1999, at a special Iftaar dinner hosted by the State Department: "Killing the innocent does not defeat terror; it feeds terror. You are making new enemies when what you need are friends."

Ms. Albright's remarks epitomize the State Department's profoundly flawed habit of emphasizing perceived or actual harms to U.S. national interests while completely ignoring ways in which U.S. policies harm and kill people in, for example, Iraq.

Both Ms. Albright and General Looney appear hell-bent on antagonizing other cultures and countries.

We ask, might they and their advisers ever develop a fresh perspective on peacemaking in the Middle East, one that emphasizes fair play, equitable trade exchanges, and advocacy for disarmament by all parties? Will we ever see serious moves toward U.S. disarmament, with acknowledgment that as long as weapon sales to Middle Eastern countries prop up the U.S. economy, each U.S. call for Iraq's disarmament sounds profoundly hollow? Will they ever hear these words as an admonishment for the U.S.: "Killing the innocent does not defeat terror; it feeds terror. You are making new enemies when what you need are friends."

A Witness to War
January 2003

I've been in Baghdad with my colleagues from Voices in the Wilderness since October 24, 2002. We are members of what we call the Iraq Peace Team, and we are intent on staying here even if George Bush dispatches the bombers, the tanks and the troops.

A few days ago, I traveled from Baghdad to Amman to meet three new members of our team. Our kind driver, Sattar, knew the road so well that he could warn me when we were approaching a bump. "Kathy, don't spill your coffee," he said.

During the drive, I told Sattar about the various news reports we'd heard following the U.N. decision to approve Resolution 1441 and the drastic disarmament terms set out by the U.N. Security Council. I was surprised that he knew so little about such an important development. He told me that he and most people he knows aren't following the news very closely. They feel responsible to maintain a semblance of ordinary life, to keep busy, so that they won't succumb to panic and the overwhelming frustrations caused by evolving news reports. "Kathy, really," he suddenly blurted, "I am so scared."

While in Amman, I watched incredulously as CNN aired a U.S. military tape showing a three-dimensional simulation of urban areas in Baghdad. Suddenly, I was seeing an accurate rendering of Abu Nuwas Street, and then the Al Fanar hotel, our home in Baghdad. The tape precisely depicts our immediate neighborhood, detailing the main intersection, walkways, buildings, and alleys. It didn't show any people. Military planners can prepare for war with precision, confidence, and an eerie certainty about "the neighborhood." But residents endure agonizing uncertainty with not a single realistic plan for survival should an attack occur.

Back in Baghdad, Lamia, an English professor at Baghdad University, didn't want to talk about impending war. She seemed relieved when I quickly changed the subject to shoptalk about teaching English as a second language. We compared notes about methods, assignments that work well, predictable problems in course work. I could have been talking with any co-worker at the community college where I last taught ESL courses—except that Lamia's classes may be suspended before the semester ends, disrupted by war.

Amal, on the other hand, doesn't hesitate to tell me what she has heard through the grapevine about U.S. war plans against Iraq. Amal has also been an English teacher at a secondary school, but she couldn't support her family on the meager salary. Now she tries futilely to dig her way out of debt by selling the paintings she creates after the children go to bed. She stays up through much of the night, depicting traditional scenes with dwindling supplies of oil paint. I timidly asked her what she anticipates if an attack comes. She is very definite. She will hire a taxi, pack what belongings she can, and flee to the north where she hopes to rent a home in the countryside, away from the many targets she believes the United States will bomb in her neighborhood.

What are the odds that an empty home awaits her, somewhere in the country? How many boxes of provisions can she load onto a taxi? How will she find water and fuel? It would be cruel and pointless to pummel her with these questions. Her imaginative drawings have sustained her family for over a year. Maybe, just maybe, her bold hopes will help them survive the coming months.

I wish some of Amal's determination could spark hope for Umm Zainab, a mother of nine living in an impoverished area of Iraq's southern port city, Basra. I've known Umm Zainab since the summer of 2000 when I lived near her home for seven weeks. Umm Zainab weeps readily, clinging to me as she trembles. "Where can we run?" she whispers. "How can we hide?" She and her neighbors fear being on the front lines of a future war.

One street to the east of Umm Zainab's home, I spotted an improvement since I'd last visited the neighborhood in June. Curbs are being built on both sides of the unpaved road. Almost every other aspect of Jumurriah's infrastructure is in disrepair, but the curbs will help keep raw sewage from flowing into homes—a welcome change. Not so far from Basra, on U.S. carriers and in U.S. bases under construction in nearby countries, the United States invests enormous sums building the infrastructures to support U.S. troop deployments in the region. Troops must be housed, fed, supplied with clean water and electricity, and equipped with state-of-the-art military gear. Sewage and sanitation systems must function properly to prevent outbreaks of disease amongst the troops.

We are building our team slowly, persuaded by a stubborn belief that where you stand determines what you see. We try to distance ourselves from both President Bush and President Hussein, believing that neither side is blameless. And we are encouraged—we feel blessed by—those who have joined us and by the steady flow of inquiries and applications, now exceeding one hundred, which have come into our Chicago office.

It's a challenge to orient new team members to the multiple uncertainties we face in Iraq. How long will the Iraqis allow our team members to remain in Iraq? How many new people can we bring into the country? If the United States launches an attack, if the government here is toppled, if U.S. troops invade and occupy city streets here or elsewhere in the country, how can we best accompany ordinary Iraqis whom we've met here? How can we communicate to the U.S. public the effects of warfare, should it occur?

Eager to show solidarity with demonstrations in Washington D.C., San Francisco, and numerous other cities on October 26, our team set to work planning our own protest in Baghdad that day. We designed an enlarged blank check to hold in front of the U.N. headquarters along with signs that said, "End Sanctions Against Iraq," and "No Blank Check for War Against Iraq." We also held a life-size photo of an Iraqi child on a banner that asked, "Is She Our Enemy?" And we cited U.N. statistics about the numbers of Iraqi children who have died as a direct result of economic sanctions.

The press that came to the demonstration outnumbered us by about five to one, and we're still smarting from the stories they filed. The dismissive tone of the stories in the *New York Times*, the *Washington Post*, the *Los Angeles Times*, and the *Chicago Tribune* have set us back considerably. Articles characterizing us as an ineffectual group of naive people in the thrall of a dictatorship belittle six years of hard work on the part of hundreds of people who have done their best to speak truthfully about their experiences while nonviolently resisting U.S.-led U.N. economic sanctions against Iraq.

One journalist called us an anemic group, referring to our small number, but failed to mention that the U.S. government threatens us with twelve years in prison for the "crime" of traveling to Iraq and for making any transaction (even buying a bottle of water) while here. In May 2002, the U.S. Office of Foreign Assets began imposing $10,000 fines on Voices in the Wilderness delegates named in a pre-penalty notice issued by that office back in 1998.

A *New York Times* article by John Burns on October 27, 2002, bore this headline: "12 Americans Stage a Protest Hussein is Happy to Allow." We joked that the article might just as easily have been entitled, "John Burns Writes an Article Bush is Happy to Read." Worse, the caption accompanying the *Times* story stated that our demonstration was held "in support of Saddam Hussein." Our work has consistently been to support the Iraqi people, not Saddam, and our press release made clear that what we were doing was challenging the

United Nations to uphold its own charter, which calls for protection of vulnerable civilian populations during times of war. People in the United States are seldom prompted to think about the cares and concerns of the twenty-four million people living in Iraq. It's as if there were only one person here, and his name was Saddam Hussein.

"Do you see yourselves as human shields?" journalists asked. We can't deter bombs or attacks any more than you can, we told them. But we can treat all human beings as equals. And we can serve as witnesses to our own government's war.

A few journalists were surprised at the negative slant toward Voices in the Wilderness and the Iraq Peace Team. "Why would someone want to smear you like that?" asked one reporter.

Members of the mainstream U.S. media insisted on asking us how we could avoid being used by the Iraqi government. But we will not let the media cast us as dupes. We reject the either/or, the with-us-or-against-us dichotomy that George W. Bush tries to impose on us all. And when I can, I try to point out to the mainstream journalists that they've succeeded enormously in informing the U.S. public about the horrors committed by the current regime in Iraq while for the most part neglecting the horrors the United States has committed. That the regime here has used chemical weapons, engaged in torture, and violated the political and civil rights of Iraqi civilians is repugnant to all who cherish human rights. And yet, what the U.S. public doesn't understand and will possibly never comprehend is that the greatest violations of human rights in Iraq since the Gulf War have happened as a result of U.S.-led U.N. economic sanctions against Iraq.

We have seen the truth of bombings and of economic sanctions, and that is why we passionately oppose the coming war against the families of Iraq.

Last night, friends working in our Chicago office (the three-bedroom apartment where I live on the city's north side) called to say that the U.S. Treasury Department has imposed a $20,000 fine on me and our campaign for the "crime" of delivering medicines and toys to Iraq. We don't believe that we've behaved as criminals. And we won't be paying any penalties. As long as the U.S. government approves big budgets for military planners, military suppliers, and military consultants, we'll claim our right to practice the works of mercy rather than support the works of war.

The road ahead is unknowable. But I find a calming inspiration in a bit of lore about Saint Francis of Assisi. During the bloody slaughter occasioned by "Christian" Crusades, Saint Francis traveled on foot for a year and risked his life to reach the sultan's tent. The sultan begged Francis to accept expensive gifts. Francis refused them but carried forth a vision of peacemaking predicated on simplicity, service, sharing, and an obstinate refusal to kill.

Imagining Survival
November 4, 2002

PERSPECTIVES—Seeing our friend, Sattar, helped me put my own frustration into perspective. His good-natured decency is legendary amongst Voices in the Wilderness and other delegations that visit Iraq. He and his brothers have safely driven us round trip from Amman to Baghdad, and between Baghdad and other cities, in over one hundred journeys over the past six years. By now, understandably, Sattar hates driving. And yet I've never seen him indulge in a sour mood. He's a well-trained civil engineer, fluent in English, capable, likeable, and utterly trustworthy. More than a decade of undeserved punishments that daily humiliate him and his family hasn't diminished his resolve to make the best of harsh, disappointing circumstances. Today he told me briefly about something that had made him particularly happy. A neighbor of his, a retired teacher, is completely blind. An entire wall of the man's home had crumbled, and if the wall wasn't rebuilt the house would become uninhabitable. Sattar and two of his friends decided to put their skills to work. Sattar paid for the bricks and the cement out of his own meager earnings. The crew worked steadily for two days to erect a new wall and refused any payment. I'm quite sure Sattar and his friends will continue looking out for this family. "To give and not count the cost"—it's an enviable accounting system.

CRIMINAL ACTS—Today, Moayed managed to tell me what is weighing on his mind every day. His baby is near death. The infant needs heart surgery and Moayed has "no falous"—no money. I hated telling him that we can't help him. His brave smile crumbled in a raw mixture of pain, disappointment, and resignation. Nearly every one of Moayed's co-workers has a needy loved one whose health requires amounts of "falous" many times greater than the income they earn working double shifts at local hotels. If we help Moayed, we'll raise the hopes of dozens more people and ultimately cause terrific envy, mistrust, and disappointment.

When President Bush first approached the U.N. to seek support for U.S. plans to "disarm Iraq," he used a line earlier delivered by Paul

Wolfowitz, Rumsfeld's number two man in the Pentagon, justifying the U.S. insistence on a right to attack Iraq by observing that Iraq's president would watch security services torture children in front of their parents. In hospitals across this country, I and many others have watched children dying in pain in front of their parents. I have held many such children in my arms and have tried to comfort their mothers with the hope that we were working to end the U.S./U.N. economic embargo that was causing their deaths.

When bombs fall on cities and villages, children are tortured in the presence of their parents. When families flee from war and end up in refugee camps, thousands of children suffer and die in the arms of their parents.

Looking at Moayed today, I can only agree with President Bush. It is a crime against humanity to knowingly and deliberately torture children in the presence of their parents. We have seen the truth of bombings and of economic sanctions, and that is why we passionately oppose the coming war against the families of Iraq.

But our passions and hopes do little right now to comfort Moayed, his wife, or his child.

And I don't know how to greet him tomorrow.

INFRASTRUCTURE—Last week, while in Basra, I visited most of the homes along a newly curbed street in the Jumurriyah neighborhood. Mothers told me that they are so frightened of being on the front lines of a full scale attack that even the sound of a warplane flying overhead triggers memories of 1991 which, in the case of one young mother, causes what she describes as a "psychological collapse." While these mothers try to adjust to constant anxiety, focusing on everyday tasks and maintaining at least a semblance of normalcy, the warlords exercise calm pragmatism as they meticulously refine plans to attack Iraq. Families quiver in Jumurriyah. Is the street where I visit, one lined with impoverished yet utterly hospitable dwellings and a curb which took years to build, in the crosshairs of the world's largest firing squad?

Mahmoud's Prayer
November 29, 2002

I've known Fatima and her brothers and sisters for six years. I first met them in August 1996. They were playing on the roof of their dilapidated home. I looked up and mistakenly thought that the youngest was about to take a tumble. It was a *Catcher in the Rye* moment, me racing to catch the child while he and his siblings giggled in amusement. They immediately swept me into their home for an afternoon full of antics and fun. Nine-year-old Fatima was in charge of her five younger brothers and sisters while her mother and two older brothers were away each day. (Karima, a widow, tried to earn money selling chewing gum and other items at the local market.)

Fatima's ability to care for the kids amazed me. I've often joined in on their zany entertainments—shadow shows, mimes, circle games, chants, and a raucous routine in which the gorgeous twin daughters grab tiny Mahmoud and swing him back and forth like a sack of potatoes. A few days ago, one of the twins donned a headscarf, grabbed my hand, and ushered me into the family's sleeping room. After instructing me to sit down, she unfolded two prayer mats, one for her and one for Mahmoud. They were proud to show me how they prayed together. Mahmoud is a beginner, not quite sure of the words and gestures, but eager to get it right. Then Fatima entered. She was intensely beautiful, just then, as she recited the prayer looking fondly at Mahmoud, careful to assure that he repeated each line correctly.

This morning, Neville Watson, a seventy-eight-year-old Australian lawyer and minister who has joined our team, taught us the Salaat, the final prayer of the day, recited by Muslims throughout the world. This is little Mahmoud's prayer as well.

O God you are peace.
From you is peace and unto you is peace.
Lord, let us live in peace.
Receive us into your peace.
To you be praise and honor. We hear and obey.
Grant us your forgiveness Lord. And unto you be our becoming.

Moayed
December 3, 2002

We finally managed to work out a way to help Moayed, whose baby, Shehadah, needs heart surgery. The surgery will happen five days from now. Doctors are hopeful that the surgery can be successful, but the post-operative care poses grave problems since the baby cannot remain in the hospital for more than a few days following the surgery.

Moayed took Nathan Musselman, another Voices in the Wilderness delegate, and me to his home in a beleaguered area of

Baghdad. "How can you describe this?" asked Nathan, who had never been to an area like this. "I mean, it's like living in a huge mud puddle." Sewage, muck, and garbage filled the street outside Moayed's home. Moayed, his wife Haifa, their baby, and Haifa's mother, who has only one leg, live together in a one-room home. They have a stand-up latrine and a two-burner gas range in a tiny patio area in front of the home. There is a huge hole above the latrine. It's hard to imagine how they manage to help Haifa's mother navigate between the latrine and the couch. She has a wheelchair, but it is broken. I asked if they had a space heater; the answer, "No falous" (no money).

Moayed spent seven years in the military during the Iran-Iraq war. He was released for two months and was then sent to Kuwait in 1990. Since the Gulf War, he has worked almost every day of his life, trying hard to be a provider. But there's simply no way that he can escape the poverty that enmeshes him and his family. Even so, he and his wife went out of their way to provide us with a generous meal and hospitality.

Power Plant
December 18, 2002

Last night we visited the Al Taji power plant. Charlie Litekey devised ingenious sand-based candles inside empty plastic water bottles and, joined by two Japanese delegations, we were a fine backdrop for Iraqi speakers. Amal Alwan, holding four-year-old Ali in her arms and flanked by her other son and daughter, spoke about how she, as a young mother about to give birth, was traumatized during the Gulf War when a nearby electrical power plant was bombed, causing the cellar in her home to cave in. She urged world powers to prevent a new war and spoke about how hard it is to protect children when war breaks out.

During a tour of the facility, the plant manager showed us two generators delivered several months ago, each costing six million dollars. Economic sanctions forbid the British company that sold them to Iraq to deliver crucial supportive items, including installment instructions and essential computer software. Experts from the U.K. company aren't allowed to come to Iraq to give Iraqi engineers the necessary training for using the new generators. There they sit, big white elephants that are a testimony to highway robbery—thievery! Iraqis have to pay, sight unseen, for any equipment they receive whether it functions or not. The U.K. company pocketed Iraq's payment. Case closed.

We wanted to remind President Bush that he has promised not to bomb sites that are crucial for civilian survival and well being. Yet even as the military buildup looms, civilian survival is undermined by the harsh and humiliating effects of the economic sanctions.

Crossing Borders
Christmas 2002

Nathan Musselman and I boarded the public bus that travels from Baghdad to Amman on Christmas Eve after an absurdly hurried packing job. Nathan had discovered, much to our dismay, that he unwittingly let his visa expire. "Sorry," said the Iraqi immigration official. "There is no chance. You must leave." Nathan's only option for remaining in Iraq where our team greatly needs his experience is to petition, from Amman, for a new visa. As for me, Chicago friends had insisted that I'm needed at home for a few weeks if we're to form new "waves" of Iraq Peace Team participants. I'd just learned that the only flight from Amman to Chicago with an available seat departs on December 26.

Last night, Nathan and I gave way, emotionally, to hapless uncertainty and near despair. We stood for hours, shivering helplessly during a seven-hour ordeal of border crossing. It was a bone-chillingly cold and damp night. We cursed our stupidity in not dressing warmly enough to weather the long hours outdoors and in unheated "reception" rooms while waiting for officials at the Iraqi and then the Jordanian border to search luggage and check papers for each of the bus passengers.

When I began visibly shaking, Rabab, a kindly English teacher from Qut, came up and draped a warm blanket over my shoulders. Then an elderly fellow stripped off his long gold-colored *abaya* and insisted that I wear it. Enfolded in their kindness, I could only smile gratefully and wish that my stilted Arabic could tell them how ironic it is that a U.S. Christian, when surrounded by unfailing Arab hospitality, has a small chance to identify with Jesus, Mary, and Joseph finding no room at the inn! Nor could I voice my sorrow over knowing that, bleak as the scene was, and it really couldn't have been more stark, the Iraqi passengers crossing out of Iraq are no doubt envied by millions of Iraqis. As a fearful cold spell of impending war, upheaval, and chaos locks in place, Iraqis dream of bundling their families into buses and taxis to reach safer terrain in any land other than Iraq.

Like thousands of people worldwide, Nathan and I would give anything to be effective, compelling antiwar voices. We despise the sinister growth of this killing machine, which uses the suffering of Iraqis under their current regime as an excuse for yet more suffering, and which hides behind fanciful euphemisms of "liberation" and "deliverance." But time is running out as the window of opportunity to avoid war seems ready to slam shut. U.S. people still don't comprehend the complexities and hardships Iraqis have faced. If the antiwar movement could instill true understanding, perhaps ordinary U.S. citizens might yet have compassion for ordinary Iraqis. Those who have succumbed to a belief that the war is wrong but unstoppable might yet be moved to risking resistance. Still, I fear there will be no room in U.S. hearts for Iraqis bracing themselves for war. I can't imagine more innocent and more defenseless people. When I return to Iraq in several weeks, their agonizing psychological burden of expectation may very well have intensified beyond what already seems unbearable.

Just now, it's a gift to remember Rabab's kindness, to feel the heavy blanket of warmth that she wrapped around me, and to stand aligned with the forgiveness that brings to life the Christmas message.

Good friends have urged me to look for hooks, when I write, with which ordinary people in the U.S. can identify. Tonight my narrative might best be understood by deportees, homeless people, and detainees. But perhaps those Christians who lit candles tonight and remembered the Christ child born in a manger, surrounded by cave dwellers, soon to be a fugitive, will hearken to a narrative begging for the light to shine in the darkness... and the darkness shall not overcome it.

Crucial Days Ahead
January 30, 2003

Nine of us arrived in Baghdad close to midnight last night. This is my twentieth trip to Iraq since our campaign began in 1996. "After the first trip, the novelty wears off," joked Thorne Anderson, as we waited several hours to clear the Jordanian and Iraqi borders. But a novel sadness awaited us as we entered a country on the verge of being attacked. At breakfast, several hotel workers whom I've known for years greeted me warmly and then asked, timidly, "There will be a war?" Another friend had a more dire view. "They are going to kill us," he said, matter-of-factly.

We began our day at a press conference held by the Center for Economic and Social Rights, during which international scholars reported on the likelihood of catastrophic humanitarian crises in Iraq should the U.S. decide to wage a new war here. Roger Normand, an international law scholar, insisted that human beings are entitled to protection under international law. Pentagon plans for high intensity bombardment in a comprehensive war would translate into severe, intensified suffering for Iraq's people. Hans von Sponeck, former U.N. Humanitarian Coordinator in Iraq, insisted that although the CESR team intended to create a war effects evaluation database, it is nevertheless crucial to assert that peace is still possible. "Iraqis want to turn a chapter in their history and prevent war," said Mr. Von Sponeck. He will remain in Iraq for two more days, working to develop peace initiatives with other humanitarian groups and "high profile" individuals.

Our team members have met for long hours working out various details, e.g., operation of an emergency back-up generator, use of the satellite phone that I carried in, emergency medical training, maintenance of files for individual declarations that, in the event of death, one prefers to be cremated than to be shipped back to the U.S. And a less dire list gives names of people who want to help set up an arts and crafts workshop for children hospitalized at a local cancer ward.

"Maybe Monday me and my family will make a well," said Sattar, our driver, as we neared Baghdad. This afternoon, the desk manager at our hotel pointed toward the open lot where hired workers were installing a well for our use. "Will you have room for more of us?" I asked. "Yes, sure," he joked, "we are making room on the rooftop."

It is too soon to answer our friends who ask if there will be a war, too soon to declare that war is inevitable. Crucial days ahead offer people throughout the world a momentous opportunity to prevent bloodshed and destruction. The novelty of such a triumph would never wear off. It could usher all of us toward the political maturity required to survive our shameful capacity for annihilation.

Border Between Heaven and Hell
March 3, 2003

On Feb. 24, twenty of us set up a four-day tent encampment in the Demilitarized Zone between Iraq and Kuwait. "Between Heaven and

Hell, that's how I felt, the whole day," said our Franciscan priest, Jerry Zawada.

When we arrived, the sky was darkening, thunder rumbling across the desert. Yet the border area, desolate and dramatic, was oddly still. Neville Watson, an Australian lawyer and Uniting Church minister, recalled the original Gulf Peace Team camp in January 1991. Then, anticipating war, our encampment on the Iraq side of the Iraq-Saudi border, was filled with futility and despair the first night of Desert Storm. Huddled together beneath the clear skies on a cold moonless night, seventy-two of us watched and listened as bombers flew overhead once every five minutes. Within three days, Iraq's electrical grid was destroyed, along with much of its crucial infrastructure. Now, twelve years later, Neville murmured, "What does it take to stop such madness? Is nothing changed?"

Yesterday we walked to the border post carrying enlarged vinyl banners bearing pictures of people we've met. From a distance it must have looked as though these friends were walking alongside us. Examining the pictures more carefully, I recognized several children from the nearby village of Abu Faloos, a forlorn little place known to us mainly because a little girl who lives there was struck by a bomb on January 25, 1999. The bomb, aimed at a fertilizer factory, missed its intended target and hit Israa as she left her school. She now has only one arm and bears large scars on her torso and belly. After we leave the border, we can bring the beautiful pictures of children from Abu Faloos to the village. What an adornment.

We're in touch with a large support network and thousands beyond—messages stream forth in hope of stopping a war. The tiny arrow we represent points to possibilities of unarmed intervention, someday—perhaps in a future when America gains political maturity.

Late last night, air raid sirens droned for several minutes. I thought of my visit several weeks ago, with a Basran friend who was confined to bed rest because of a difficult pregnancy. She and her children live on the second floor of a small, cramped dwelling. "My children—they hear siren and they seize me. They insist, they want me to come downstairs. And I tell them, 'No, there is no difference between upstairs and downstairs. There is protection only in Allah and Allah is everywhere.'" And so it goes. The massive capacity for destruction on the other side of this border can erupt across this very road where we now sit, damning many thousands to hellfire in the weeks ahead.

Vulnerable, unarmed, without the slightest desire to bring harm to American people, a haven of innocence dwells in neighborhoods, throughout villages and cities, on this side—on the cusp of Heaven and Hell.

Shock and Awe
March 20, 2003

Jeremy Scahill, a journalist who'd been with us until just before the war began, called at 3:00 a.m. on March 20 to tell us that the planes had taken off. By 5:00 a.m., after having gathered our members and waited two hours, we wondered if it was a false alarm. No one panicked; we convinced Neville to let us into the emergency rations to distribute a few bags of M&M chocolate-covered peanuts, we made many cups of tea, and we calmly chatted with one another in Neville's large and comfortable room. We wandered back to our rooms, eager to catch up on sleep. At 5:30 a.m., explosions began. I shuddered—Jeremy was right after all. The explosions were on the outskirts of the city, and we learned later that the U.S. had bombed a bunker, thinking Saddam Hussein was there.

Later in the day, traffic was heavy, the markets were full, and people went about their business. I held on to some optimism that the war would be short, the attacks pinpointed on military targets in remote areas.

Our phones rang constantly as reporters from all over the world called to ask for our reactions to the onset of war. By day three (dubbed A-Day in Pentagon parlance—the *Army Times* reported that the U.S. military used every type of aircraft it had), the bombings were much closer to our area, and from then on bombings occurred without cease.

Often you could feel the floors shudder and hear the windows rattle. We were relieved when it seemed the hotel building could withstand the attacks. When an ear-splitting, gut-wrenching blast would shake the building, you could see the younger kids quickly checking the adults' faces. If the adults seemed calm, the kids would note it and go on with play, games, meals, and conversations. I think all of us were trying to physically control flinching responses. Frequently, the response of Iraqi friends would be a clicking of the tongue, then "Laish, laish?"—Why, why?

I felt dismay, deep sadness, anger—but also a familiar sense of intense determination not to let the bombs have the last word.

Generally, I'd try to set aside whatever I was doing or disengage from whatever conversation I was in to scoop up little Miladh and Zaineb, the youngest of the Al Fanar's residents, whenever they'd appear. With their mother, they stayed overnight in the bomb shelter and also had a room on one of the floors above. Once the little ones got over initial shyness, it was easy to enter into their lives. At age three, Miladh was delicate, rambunctious, and clever. Her sister Zaineb, one-and-a-half, would reach out her arms and run toward me each time we saw each other. Shadow shows, counting games, dances, songs—all of us invented ways to help distract the little girls from the war's tension. Their mom would sometimes feel so overcome by grief and fear for her loved ones, especially her brothers in Najaf, about whom she'd had no news, that she'd need time alone, to sob. When you feel helpless to stop the planes that roar overhead and unleash murderous destruction below, it's a huge relief to at least help one young mother care for her lovely daughters. But quite honestly, these two captivated me so much that I'd become distracted from the war or any feelings of responsibility to our team. It was mutually beneficial.

Abu Zaineb, their father, was the desk manager for the overnight shift. Often one of the girls would awaken during an attack. Sometimes I'd cradle one and he the other, hoping their mom could get some sleep. I walked the hallways many nights, with one of the girls in my arms, singing a lullaby, telling them how beautiful they were, whispering words to "We Shall Overcome" in Arabic, or singing, in Arabic, the hymn "O Finlandia"—but soon after the bombing began, both little girls were grinding their teeth, morning, noon, and night.

As for our team, we'd discuss ways to keep opposing the war, keep building relationships with the ordinary Iraqis who had welcomed us into their families while our country bombed the living daylights out of their neighborhoods, terrifying their children and setting the stage for ongoing misery. I told team members that if I returned to the U.S., I'd take the opposition to a military base as soon as possible.

While the phones were working, we could call friends and families in different parts of the city to check up on them. Occasionally, we'd walk over to visit families, or they'd come to us. Sometimes we'd scramble out of a home very quickly, if an attack had begun.

Sometimes a siren would wail before or after an attack, but really, it was impossible to know whether it announced a warning or an "all-clear." An attack might last for ten minutes, but some would continue for over an hour. In the first days of the war, a muezzin's prayer call would be sung from mosques all over Baghdad, after every attack. When the electricity went out, we missed that response.

At the Al Fanar hotel, people congregated in a tearoom, in a small restaurant, and in the lobby. The Muslim owner's extended family was there, along with the extended family of his neighbor, made up of Christians.

Early in the morning, several members of our team would meet for an hour of prayer, music, and reflections. Eventually the entire team would gather, taking time to check up on one another, share news heard over short-wave radio, and decide how much movement we'd attempt to make within Baghdad. Our meetings were often punctuated with the sound of blasts and explosions.

Much of my day was spent visiting with people in the hotel. I'd known some of the hotel staff for many years and had been with them during the 1998 Desert Fox bombing. With only a skeletal crew, they didn't mind if we traipsed in and out of the kitchen to help out or fill our thermoses with boiled water. The Christian family's grandfather, a lawyer who spoke English, was a walking history book. Young teenagers were absorbed with playing board games ("Risk" was especially popular), helping us with our fledgling Arabic efforts, racing up and down the stairs, probably finding the whole strange scene a bit adventurous. One evening, I headed down to the bomb shelter looking for Cynthia Banas and came upon two burly young men, each laying on cots with their heads in their mothers' laps, who were stroking their curly-haired heads. They all grinned at me, and then we collapsed in laughter.

Cathy Breen was in the room next to me, Neville down the hall. Whenever a blast seemed nearby, in the middle of the night, we'd usually poke our heads out to check on one another. Often we'd give up on sleep and sit in the hallway, chatting.

When the electricity went out, all across Baghdad, we'd gather by candlelight in the tearoom, at night, for hushed conversations. The Iraqi adults told us about their experiences during successive wars, their views about why the U.S. was going to war, who was to blame— sometimes the hotel owner would give a wry glance at Saddam's picture, but all agreed that war wasn't the answer.

The Illness of Victors
March 19, 2003

I suppose I'm more prepared than most of my companions for the grueling roar of warplanes, the thuds that threaten eardrums, the noise of anti-aircraft and exploding "massive ordnance." Compared to average Iraqis my age, I've tasted only a small portion of war, but I'm not a complete stranger, having spent nights under bombardment here in Iraq during the 1991 Gulf War, in Sarajevo in 1992, in the 1998 Desert Fox bombing, and last spring in the Jenin camp on the West Bank. I feel ready to insist with passion that war is never an answer. But nothing can prepare me or anyone else for what we could possibly say to the children who will suffer in the days and nights ahead. What can you say to a child who is traumatized, or maimed, or orphaned, or dying? Perhaps only the words we've murmured over and over at the bedsides of dying children in Iraqi hospitals. "I'm sorry. I'm so very sorry."

One of my fondest childhood memories is that of holding my baby brother, Jerry, and pointing his gaze toward a beautiful sunset. I wanted him to feel the awe I felt. I was a pious child, capable of great awe when genuflecting before the candle lit altar in our neighborhood church. Now the world's greatest killing machine perversely appropriates the preserve of sacred awe as a sick smokescreen for inflicting terror.

Readying for the "Shock and Awe" coming our way, I've turned to David Dellinger's accounts of travel in North Vietnam when the U.S. was strafing villages, mutilating civilians, and burning the earth. My beloved Karl says that Dellinger may be one of the finest human beings that has ever walked on our planet. I agree. Dellinger hated to see "just normal people" suffering from the illness of getting "pleasure" by harming people. It isn't just the suffering of the victims that upsets him, but also the illness of the victors. We must labor to cure that illness.

It's a sad and tragic irony that on the eve of warfare we can presume that today may be the last day of the cruel, perverse sanctions regime. *Now we'll bomb you so that we can stop starving you.*

"Embedded media" traveling with U.S. troops will no doubt show footage of Iraqis celebrating release from a brutally repressive regime, of horrible weapons caches discovered by advancing U.S. troops. Years of murderous suffering preceding and following the "Shock and Awe" operation aren't likely to preoccupy the victors whose illness goes undiagnosed in their antiseptic think tank settings.

But the momentum, globally, for curing the warlords, has grown substantially during this dramatic and critical time. "Ring the bell that still can ring. Forget your perfect offering," croons Leonard Cohen in his song "Anthem." "There is a crack in everything. That's how the light gets in. That's how the light gets in."

Relative Calm in the Midst of War
March 20, 2003

People in our team here are heartened by news of actions in the United States to continue antiwar momentum. The bombings last night were intense for about thirty minutes beginning at 9:10 p.m. But, compared to what people were bracing themselves for, which was the "Shock and Awe," these attacks have seemed limited. We're getting rumors and some hard news, mostly from journalists who tell us what seems to be going on.

Today I had a chance to go and visit families in three different neighborhoods, each eerily calm. There is still not much in the way of a military presence on the streets other than sand bags piled up at various intersections.

I visited Umm Rend's home where five women have survived for over a decade on the meager earnings of two women who are schoolteachers. They begged us not to leave. Umm Rend's tiny mother clung to me, saying, "Please, tell me, where I hide?" They are quite close to what I think is a military storage depot. In spite of their slim rations, they insisted we must return and eat with them.

And then there is Karima's family. They have just now come to visit us at the hotel. This is the family I am the most worried about. They are in a precarious spot, and their neighbors seem to know it. Many of them have left by now. I hope the hotel owner will allow them to stay with us, but . . .

It is almost impossible for me to imagine how Chicagoans where I live would react if they experienced the bombing attacks of the past night and morning. If people known to be from the attacking country were in Chicago, would they be so readily welcomed in ordinary households as we are here?

Spring Morning: After "Shock and Awe"
March 22, 2003

Here in Baghdad, along the Tigris River, a gentle dawn and the sweetest of birdsongs were more precious than ever following a horrific night of intense bombardment. With the calm morning came relief after learning that the families of friends who work at the hotel are okay. Abu Hassan, a pro at charades, pantomimed what happened in his home. He pointed to the windows in my room, held up five fingers, touched the floor, and then affirmed, "Finished." Five windows had shattered. Then he swung his arms around to imitate a ceiling fan, also "finished," it had crashed to the floor, and next he crouched down with his hands on his head to indicate what the children had done. Riyadh then told us that his brother and father were "finished" in the 1991 Gulf War—making a gesture of falling asleep, which meant that both had been killed, and then he mimicked wiping tears from his eyes to explain that his mother had wept through the night, remembering past agony while quivering through the present one. Abu Hassan and Riyadh live in the impoverished Saddam City section of Baghdad.

At 8:00 p.m. last evening, I sat on a second floor balcony of our hotel watching tracer lights flash across the sky. The first round of bombing seemed distant and in the calm that followed, Neville suggested that perhaps that would be it for tonight. We joked about Neville's prediction, quite exact, that bombing would begin precisely 45 minutes after he lay down to take a nap. "You'll just have to stay awake now Neville," said Ed. Our levity was broken by thunderous explosions that repeatedly shook our hotel.

I darted to my room, swiftly poured a cup of coffee, pocketed a handful of cotton swabs, grabbed my journal and a few books, and then hurried down two flights of stairs to join other hotel residents and staff in the ground floor "tearoom."

I saw Marwan, age twelve, and his nine-year-old sister, Dima, surveying the adults' faces. Thankfully, all of us were managing to appear calm, and Marwan and Dima followed suit. A Christian woman made the sign of the cross while a Muslim man unrolled his prayer mat (the hotel owner, a Muslim, has invited his Christian neighbors to stay with us).

We settled in to endure a long night of bludgeoning attacks on Baghdad. The cotton swabs were handy for playing pick-up sticks and making a tic-tac-toe grid. Cathy Breen produced a few lumps of clay, which we made into markers. Mohammed, our friendly cab driver, picked up a tiny pink lump and popped it in his mouth, expecting it to be a gumdrop. Did he do it on purpose? Anyway, it was a brilliant distraction that sent the children into gales of laughter.

Tomorrow we'll plan a birthday party for Amal, who turns thirteen. Last night, a cake appeared in the tearoom in celebration of Mother's Day. Tiny Zainab and Miladh, daughters of the hotel night manager, have warmed up to me and let me help their parents rock them to sleep. And so it goes. As Operation Iraq Freedom storms on, we'll liberate ourselves from any government's efforts to sever natural bonds between us.

As I write, I can hear explosions in the distance. Clouds of smoke are billowing in every direction. We've heard that last night's casualty list includes 207 wounded, four of whom died in hospitals. News reports say that more than 1,000 Cruise missiles were launched last night, and the U.S. may be planning to release many more tonight. On a beautiful spring day, welcome to Hell.

Angry, Very Angry
March 25, 2003

I'm surrounded by some of the most kindly and gentle people in the world, coming from many walks of life. Members of our Iraq Peace Team have "checked in" on most days of our five-month stay here, some having been here for the full five months, and continually give expression to sentiments that are sacred in their affirmation of simplicity, sharing, and commitment to nonviolence. But in the last several days, feelings of intense anger have surfaced. "I'm angry," confided Sang Jin Han, of South Korea, a peace activist who has led South Korea's campaign to ban land mines and who works closely with the Asian Peace Alliance. "I think this war will kill thousands of people."

Likewise, Zefira Hourfani, a Canadian of Algerian origin, says she is very angry, so much so that she no longer considers herself a Canadian. "Now I am an Arab," she says, "and I am angry at the western countries."

Lisa Ndjeru, a Rwandan woman, also a Canadian citizen, took particular umbrage over President Bush's request that Americans help the U.S. troops by assisting them with home repair and childcare. "What lunacy!" said Lisa. "Young Americans whose children need care and whose homes are falling apart should loan themselves to destroy homes and maim children in this country in order to finally get some help?"

We try not to take our anger out on journalists who contact us. Neville Watson is normally gracious and entirely rational when he speaks to media. But he confessed that a few days ago, he "let him have it with both barrels" when an Australian "shock-jock" referred to civilian casualties as the expected collateral damage that comes with war. "How dare you refer to our friends as 'collateral damage'?" asked Neville. "And who is Mr. Bush kidding when he expects us to believe that the U.S. wants to secure Iraq's oil fields for the benefit of Iraqi people?" Neville goes on to recite the sad and sordid history of economic siege and warfare that has already cost the lives of hundreds of thousands of children under age five.

Yes, we are angry, very angry, and yet we feel deep responsibility to further the nonviolent antiwar efforts that burgeon in cities and towns throughout the world. We can direct our anger toward clear confrontation, controlling it so that we won't explode in reactionary rage, but rather draw the sympathies of people toward the plight of innocent people here who never wanted to attack the U.S., who wonder, even as the bombs terrify them, why they can't live as brothers and sisters with people in America.

The Bush administration says the war has been successful because so far there have been only 500 casualties. From our March 24, 2003 report on visits to the Yermouk and Al Kindy hospital trauma centers, where hundreds of wounded and maimed patients have been treated over the past five days, here are some of the success stories:

Roesio Salem, age ten, is from Hai Risal. She went to the entrance of her home on the first day of the attack and shouted to her father, "Bomb coming!" at which point she was hit. She is ten years old and has sustained severe chest injuries.

We couldn't take our eyes off the gentle girl as she smiled at us from her hospital bed.

Fatima, ten years old, from Radwaniya, suffered multiple fractures when she and her family ran from their home in an urban area on Friday evening, March 21. A wall fell down and she suffered a fractured tibia. The family had no means of transport and had to wait until the next morning to get her to a hospital. Her father, Abu Mustafa, who works as a farm laborer, said, "We are like brothers and sisters to people in the United States. We don't attack American people. Please give this message to American people. This is an invasion; it has nothing to do with democracy."

Ahmed Sabah, age eighteen, from the Al Zafrania district, was inside his home at 9:30 p.m. on Thursday, March 20. He suffered multiple wounds and a fractured arm and leg from shell fragments. An external fixator sets his compound fractures. His father asked us to show people in all peace-loving countries that his son is a victim and not a criminal.

Hamed Kathem, age twenty, sustained injuries to his leg and arteries from shelling. He was in the courtyard of his home in El Biladiya on March 20. "We haven't gone to the U.S. to hit them. They came here. Last night children were admitted to this hospital," said Hamed. And then he simply asked, "Why?" "God save all the people," said his father, quietly, "and God save all countries from this destruction."

Khadem Wadi, age sixty-three, of Saddam City, was shopping for his family on March 23, at 5:00 p.m. when shrapnel punctured his intestine and wounded his leg. Two shells were removed from his abdomen.

Hosam Khaf, a thirteen-year-old boy from Baghdad Jeddidah, was injured on Friday, March 21, at 9:00 p.m. He sustained a shell injury to his abdomen and now has a colostomy bag. He is in great pain today. He lives in a multiple-story building. As huge bombs exploded nearby, his family fled their flat. When he went into the street he was hit by shelling. His father, Abu Hosam, says, "Most of the casualties are children, elderly people, and civilians. What do they have to do with fighting and war?"

We felt some relief in being able to tell patients and their families that people in countries around the world are turning out for massive demonstrations against the war.

Each of these victims whose bedsides we visited today will lie still, hopefully recovering, with many hours to reflect on what has happened to them. Peace activists who continue to fill jails in the U.S. will likewise spend hours of confinement, pained by the cruel stupidity of warfare. Most of us are angry, very angry. Few of us can manage the genuine sweetness of little Ruba whose gaze radiated easy affection in spite of her trauma—and yet I believe that we can channel our anger, our disappointment, our frustration, and our rage into the kind of energy that will champion nonviolent resistance to the works of war, and an ever-deepening desire for the works of mercy.

Defensive Shield Revisited
April 1, 2003

Cathy Breen and I visited Amal at the home of her friends, having heard that her home had been further destroyed by ongoing bombing. She then took us to her house, which faces the river, graced by a garden where flowers are blossoming. Picking our way through broken glass at the entrance, we entered what was once one of the most well-appointed homes in Baghdad. The rooms are in disarray. Several walls are cracked, the windows are all shattered, and a thick layer of dust and grime covers the exposed furniture, books, carpets, and floors.

"It was my silly feeling," Amal said matter-of-factly, "that this will not happen. I did not move anything." She emphasized several times that neighbors could have removed everything in the past two days. "The house is open. The whole area knows about it. But nobody moved anything." Amal wasn't in her home when the windows shattered and the doors were blown out. "By chance, that night, I forgot my key and for that reason I stayed with my friends." Ten minutes after we arrived at her home, the U.S. began bombing. "They are starting it again," sighed Amal. "We should go very quickly."

We rejoined Amal's friends, two sisters who, like Amal, are elderly, scholarly, staunch, and furious. I first met them in the summer of 2002, when they invited me to tell a gathering of two dozen or so Iraqi friends about my experiences in April 2002 inside the Jenin Camp in the West Bank, just after Israeli troops had used overwhelming military force to destroy hundreds of homes in a civilian neighborhood. Amal and her friends were deeply angered when I showed them enlarged pictures of homes in the Jenin Camp that were reduced to rubble. They said they've always felt intense grief for the Palestinians who've suffered under occupation. It was unthinkable then, that Amal herself would become homeless and face life under occupation less than a year later.

"It is so unfair," said Amal. "From the simplest people to the highest people, all have suffered." Later that night, we learned that *Voice of America* radio had confirmed that an Iraqi military officer had approached a U.S. military checkpoint in Iraq appearing to be a cab driver wishing to surrender. The driver had detonated a load of explosives inside the cab, killing himself and four U.S. soldiers.

Amal has paid a high price for guessing wrongly about whether or not the U.S. would wage a massive attack against Iraq. She didn't bother to safeguard her impressive collection of valuable artwork, books, and other belongings. She and her friends aren't guessing now. They are positive that U.S. war-makers will pay a lethal and grisly price for any attempts to overtake and occupy Iraq. "We will lose the battle, but the U.S. is not the winner," she vowed. "The children talk about the monster coming. We will push back the monster, with our hands."

After Shock and Awe ended, about a week into the Occupation, on the day that Neville Watson, our oldest and wisest member, had left for Amman, I cried for a long time. Neville had steadied us, guided us. I don't recall having wept before then, but I'd stored up plenty of grief.

Dancing Days Are Done
April 15, 2003

Twenty-five years ago, I was arrested for the first time when I joined Karl Meyer and a small band of friends from our neighborhood for an action protesting draft registration at the main post office in Chicago. We were charged with disturbing the peace when we went to the window where young men submitted their draft registrations and sang an Irish ballad, "Johnny, I Hardly Knew You." The verses tell of a widow's sorrow as she beholds her Johnny, a maimed soldier conscript whose arms, eyes, and legs are gone. "Where are your legs that used to run? I fear your dancing days are done. You haven't an arm, you haven't a leg. You'll have to be put with a bowl to beg."

The widow concludes: "They're rolling out the guns again, but they'll never take our sons again. No, they'll never take our sons again. Yes, Johnny, I'm swearing to you."

I spent a little time today with Jamilla Abbas, the aunt of twelve-year-old Ali Ismayal who lies in a ward of the Al Kindy hospital, armless, with third degree burns covering his torso and abdomen. Today he awakened, crying, and asked his aunt, "Am I going to stay like this all my life?" Jamilla is now his closest relative. She is the one who must help him understand that his mother and father, his brothers and sisters are all dead.

Dr. Hameed Hussain Al-Araji told us that Ali's prognosis is grim. Septicemia has set in, and he won't be able to sustain the necessary anesthetics for the doctors to perform needed plastic surgery.

Dancing days are also done for the doctors who tend Ali and other patients at the Al Kindy hospital. Dr. Al-Araji said, "I've spent a quarter of a century as a doctor working under war."

"Speak for yourself," interrupted his colleague, Dr. Mohammed. "For me, even longer."

Dr. Al-Araji nodded, and continued. "Psychologically, emotionally, we are adjusted. We ourselves are not frightened. Just our families and our children. I will bring my family here, to be with me, so that I can work." Dr. Al-Araji was on the front in the Iran-Iraq war for four years, when he was in his thirties. He did his post-graduate work in Basra, helping heal handicapped survivors of that war. He was in Tikrit during the Gulf War in 1991. "There were many casualties, many died," he said. "In 1998, I was here. It becomes like usual for us, and this is abnormal. Certainly it affects our psychology. If you take me now to the United States and invite me to a dancing party, I cannot accept."

President Bush and his advisors envisioned Iraqis dancing in the streets, bearing flowers, to welcome the U.S. liberators. Do they need background music to expose the contradictions in their claims? My suggestion: that same Irish ballad, "Johnny, I hardly knew you."

Other Hearts
April 15, 2003

Nurses are digging graves in front of the Al Mansour Hospital. Plumes of smoke are rising from the campus of Baghdad University. Other disasters loom, as the Red Cross warns that Baghdad's medical system is in complete collapse. "Water first, and then freedom," said one Iraqi man on a BBC report this morning.

Two musicians, Majid Al-Ghazali and Hisham Al- Sharaf, came to our hotel four days ago, hoping to call relatives outside Iraq on a satellite phone. Hisham's home was badly damaged during the war. "One month ago, I was the director of the Baghdad Symphony Orchestra," Hisham said with an ironic smile. "Now, what am I?"

We joked that he could direct the telephone exchange as he tinkered with our satellite phone's solar powered battery. I told Majid we had some sheet music and a guitar for him. "What are notes?" he said, "We don't even remember."

Majid had endured a particularly rough experience. During the first week of bombing, a neighbor called the secret police and turned him in for visiting with foreigners. He was jailed the next day. After the "fall" of Baghdad, the same neighbor claimed he was actually part of the secret police. Majid is terrified now. "I think they want my house," he said. "No place is safe." He put his head in his hands.

I met Hisham at the Baghdad School of Folk Music and Ballet, in January 2002. Hisham and Majid, both graduates of the school, taught there in the daytime and rehearsed with the orchestra at night. Knowing how busy Hisham was, I felt presumptuous about suggesting a project for him and his students. I told him how meaningful the song "O Finlandia" has been to many people in the U.S. At least 150 families who lost loved ones on 9/11 had used this peace anthem as part of memorial services. Sibelius composed the melody in the late 19th century. Following World War I, people wrote lyrics emphasizing the common aspirations and dreams shared by all humanity.

Hisham chuckled and couldn't resist pointing out the irony that someone from the U.S. wanted to teach his students a peace song. "O.K.," said he, "Sing it for me. We can do this." Within two days, an entire class was singing an Arabic transliteration of the song.

Saying goodbye to Majid and Hisham that morning, I felt a wave of sadness, wondering if the hopeful, idealistic verses might embitter them now.

The next morning they returned, shaken and distraught. They had approached U.S. soldiers the previous evening asking for help to protect their school from looters. The soldiers said it was not their job and ordered Hisham and Majid to go away. They went to the entrance of the school hoping they could somehow protect it alone. Five armed men arrived. Majid, Hisham, and Hisham's brother pled with them not to attack the school. The looters argued, "We are simple people. Poor people. Soon there will be no food, no money, and we have no jobs. You are rich people."

"Please," Majid said, "we will give you the instruments, give you the furniture, but don't destroy the music, the records, the history." "No," the armed men said. "Baghdad is finished." They ransacked the school, broke many instruments, burnt the music and the records.

Why do desperate people commit deplorable acts of mindless destruction? I don't know. But some truths help offer perspective. Every day, we who enjoy superfluous, inordinate wealth and comforts, while others live in abject poverty, are ransacking the precious and irreplaceable resources of our planet. We are quickly burning up all the available fossil fuels that were created over four billion years of the planet's history. Our obscene obsession with creating weapons has cost trillions of dollars that should have been spent to meet human needs.

Through decades of warfare and sanctions, powerful elites in Iraq, the U.S., and the U.K. ignored millions of Iraq's impoverished people. Hundreds of thousands of children bore excruciating punishment and then died. Very few people cared.

"Here," Hisham said, "listen to this. This is all we have left." He handed me headphones borrowed from a Norwegian television correspondent. The taped orchestra was playing "O Finlandia." Listening to the children craft their music, I softly sang the words: "This is my song, O God of all the nations. A song of peace for lands afar and mine. This is my home, the country where my heart is. Here are my dreams, my hopes, my holy shrine. But other hearts in other lands are beating, with hopes and dreams as deep and true as mine." Then I stopped. Hisham had begun to cry.

This Is Your Country Now
April 21, 2003

I'm sitting in Amman now because of Sattar. Yesterday morning, he drove me here from Baghdad. Silently, we passed through the shattered and wrecked streets. It was his story that persuaded me to leave.

For three weeks, we had waited anxiously for news about Sattar who, since 1996, has been our closest Iraqi companion. What a relief, four days ago, to see him finally walk into the hotel lobby. "Please, Sattar," I begged, "Share some of the oranges and dates we have upstairs." "Thank you," he said, "but I am fasting." He didn't tell us exactly what motivated his fast, nor would he disclose details about the swollen knob on his forehead.

When the war began, he took his family to live with relatives outside of Baghdad. After several days, he returned to check on the family home. A missile had hit a house nearby, and two brothers were missing. Sattar went to the Saddam Hospital in the impoverished and dangerous Al Thawra neighborhood to look for them. "I found it terrible," he said. "Many, many people were asking for help. One family with five injured people had gone from place to place, seeking help, and by the time they came to this hospital, five of the family members were dead. I was coming to ask about two, but I thought, here there are so many, all needing help, so I asked a doctor if he could use me."

Sattar joined thirteen volunteers who assisted three physicians as they tended hundreds of patients. "At first, I just helped to bring the medicines and move patients. You know, always before, I could not even look when people suffer blood and wounds. But I began to learn how to insert IV injections. I could clean wounds and wrap bandages." He worked at the hospital for twelve days. "There is one doctor, his name is Thamer," said Sattar, with a measure of awe, "and he stayed in the operating room for two days and nights, without a break, performing seventy-five emergency operations. We heard gunfire outside, but fortunately several sheiks and imams were able to protect the hospital."

"If you go to that hospital you can see many pictures in one moment," he continued. "Some people trying to kill, some people trying to steal, some people trying to help by cleaning the hospital, making food, and delivering patients, some sheiks and imams giving advice."

Some western reporters came to the hospital and talked with Sattar. An interviewer pressed the idea that Iraqis should be grateful for liberation. Sattar attempted to explain how much suffering he'd seen, but the reporter insisted on a positive spin. Sattar said, "Leave now."

His eyes welled up with tears when describing what he saw on the roads while driving in Baghdad. "I saw myself many tanks protecting the Ministry of Oil. They need the maps, the information. But they do nothing to help the people, the hospitals, or the food storage. American companies are already trying to repair the oil refineries so that they can produce two million to six million barrels per day; this will bring the price of oil down. They can control the price of oil to serve American interests."

He also encountered a U.S. tank in front of a huge storage site, where one to two years' worth of grain and rice were stored. He heard a U.S. officer with a Kuwaiti accent order the tank to blast open the entrance and then tell people standing there, "Take what you need. Then you can burn it."

After twelve days, Sattar returned to his family to let them know he was all right and to bring his brother Ali back to Baghdad. At a checkpoint, a U.S. soldier questioned him. "I was wearing blue jeans and, trying to be friendly, he touched my pant leg and said, 'These are good.' I told him, 'Yes, but these were made in China, not in America.'" The soldier, surprised that Sattar spoke English, asked him, "Are you glad that we're here?"

"I said, 'No'—again, Sattar's eyes filled with tears—'I wish I could have killed before you could destroy us. You have destroyed our homes, and our 'big home.' (Baghdad). Now you should go home.'"

His brother tried to restrain him. "Are you crazy?" asked Ali. "What are you saying?"

The soldier told Sattar, "I could shoot you now."

"Yes," said Sattar, "You can do it. Nobody can do anything to you. You are strong now, but wait three months. After that, what will you tell the people? You can't manage the situation yourselves. You can't protect the civilians from themselves."

Like many Baghdadis, Sattar is mystified about what happened to the Republican Guard and the regime in Baghdad. "Umm Qasr is a small village. They could resist for fifteen days. Can you imagine that all the power in Baghdad couldn't resist for two days?"

He was silent for a few bleak moments. "Nothing has changed," he said. "Only Saddam has gone away."

"Sattar," I asked, "what will you do now?"

"Tomorrow," he said, "I will go to Jordan and start driving again."

I winced. A talented, courageous and kindly man, a well-educated civil engineer aching to use his skills, one who never joined the Baath party, who strove for over a decade to preserve the simple values of his faith and culture, must return to work as a driver, fetching more Westerners to rebuild his war-torn country.

"Well, Sattar," said Cathy Breen forlornly, "now you won't have so many problems helping Americans cross the border."

"You are right," said Sattar. "This is your country now."

Shortly after Sattar left, Cathy Breen and I decided to pack our bags.

Thomas Paine once said, "My country is the world. My religion is to do good." I don't want a country. But enormous work lies ahead, in the United States, trying to convince people that our over-consumptive and wasteful lifestyles aren't worth the price paid by people we conquer.

When we reached the Abu Ghraib dairy farming area, while driving out of Iraq, a terrible stench filled the air. We're told that many corpses of humans and cattle littered the ground of this area. It was on that stretch of the road that we passed a long line of U.S. Army vehicles, headlights on, arriving to replace the Marines. The olive green convoy resembled a funeral procession. I felt a wave of relief that Voices in the Wilderness companions remain in Baghdad. Sometime, in the not so distant future, I hope to rejoin them. But, for now, I must find a way to say, clearly, "No, Sattar, Iraq is not my country."

Where Is Madame Cynthia?
April 30, 2003

Kassem lives at the Al Monzer Hotel in Amman, where he is treated always with affection and respect. I feel puzzled not to know many details about him, though I've known him for years. Every time we'd enter the hotel, coming or going from Iraq, often in a great hurry, we took it for granted that this huge giant, a former Iraqi professor recovering from an illness that impairs his speech, this delightful character with deep pouches beneath his large, beautiful eyes, would take us into the slow motion of his life, pronouncing carefully each syllable of welcome. Last week, he radiated a familiar childlike happiness when Cathy Breen and I returned from Iraq. But his first words were, "Where is Madame Cynthia?"

"She's in Baghdad," I said. "They love her so much. How can she leave?"

"Of course," he said, nodding. "She must stay. Good."

Cynthia Banas, a seventy-two-year-old librarian from Vernon, New York, has spent decades working for peace. Her work has taken her to beleaguered communities in Central America and Haiti. With Voices in the Wilderness she has joined forty-day fasts, spent many nights in New York City jails, and helped lead delegations to break the economic sanctions on Iraq. This was her first time living in a war zone. Without fail, she flinched at each explosion. "What are we going to do?" I whispered to Cathy after the first day of the war. "Cynthia's liable to have a heart attack." Cynthia's heartbeat is strong as ever, but yes, each blast struck her deep in her heart's core. Mortars, anti-aircraft fire, cluster bombs, land mines, cruise missiles, Massive Ordnance Air Bombs, the roar of C-130 transports, JDAMs, Rocket Propelled Grenades—each and every one of the murderous, ugly attacks on human decency ripped into her mind and heart, and she cringed. She is the bravest woman I know.

When the U.S. troops arrived, outside the Al Fanar Hotel, Cynthia quickly scooped up banners for us to hold, stating, "Courage for Peace, Not War" and "War = Terror." We stared at the Marines, young men laden with many pounds of gear and weapons. They were sweaty, tired, thirsty and friendly. "Where are you from?" they shouted to us. "Are you a Red Sox fan?" "They're just kids," Cynthia observed, and within minutes she was walking toward an Armored Personnel Carrier, carrying a six-pack of bottled water.

Two days later, Cynthia approached the kid soldiers again, carrying a sign that quoted the Geneva Accords, which state that an Occupying Force is responsible to maintain law and order. Ever the librarian, she had the exact document at her fingertips.

When Cathy Breen and I packed our bags to leave Iraq, Cynthia had planned to go with us, but I wasn't surprised when she changed her mind. Raad, a young and brilliant professor of architecture and engineering, had come to tell her about a special project for which he needed her help. Before the war began, he had set April 24 as the due date for students to turn in model bridges. "They can learn so much that is useful," he told Cynthia, "constructing these models. It requires creativity. They use spaghetti noodles, scraps of cardboard, twine...but they will begin to understand many things about stresses and tensions, about the importance of details, about solving problems. And they need to care about such things now more than ever." Raad decided that he would somehow notify his students that as far as he was concerned their projects were still due. He had already visited a poor neighborhood where many of his students could pass the message through word of mouth. "Tell everyone you can," he said, finding one student, "that they should bring their projects to me." He planned to make a radio announcement in hopes of reaching more students. And he especially wanted Cynthia to witness and welcome their efforts.

Hisham Sharaf, of the Iraqi National Orchestra, also encouraged Cynthia to stay. Months ago, she had marked April 21 on our calendar: Spring concert, Iraq National Orchestra. She wouldn't miss it for the world. We often sighed, looking at that calendar as the war raged. No spring concert this year. Hisham Sharaf came to us after the war with daily updates of new destruction that had wrecked his hopes of ever again creating music with his colleagues. Like so many Iraqis I know, it seemed that his bright, gleaming, dark eyes had a changed hue lighter, akin to the soft brown of deerskin. An ineffable sadness had set in as he told us that he was too tired to attempt rebuilding his dreams again. He'd seen too much destruction following too many battles. On the afternoon of the day Cynthia had packed her bags, Hisham came back to tell her that he'd changed his mind. The concert was postponed, not canceled. Could Cynthia plan to attend?

At 7:30 each morning, throughout the bombing, we gathered for reflection, taking turns to offer a prayer, a story, a favorite poem or reading, and, often, music. Cynthia loves music as she loves life. Neville had come equipped with marvelous tapes. Frequently, we listened to a song from *Les Miserables*. "Take my hand and point me to tomorrow.... To love another person is to see the face of God." Cynthia would close her eyes, a soft smile on her face. Almost inevitably, a blast would startle her.

Here in Chicago, we're working to produce new literature defining our future campaign efforts. We want to continue voicing cares and concerns of ordinary Iraqi people. We feel sure that preventing a "next" war requires effectively countering the present war propaganda. Honestly, I'm not sure how to answer the question, "Where is the peace movement?" But as we hold fast to the fact that the critical mass needed to prevent a war before it starts was almost attained, let's also be confident that answers will come if we join Kassem, our beloved Iraqi refugee at the Al Monzer Hotel, and simply ask, "Where is Madame Cynthia?" Iraqis begged Cynthia to stay. I believe that she'll return, but not before she raises her voice, here, to insist that war and occupation are not the answer.

Testimony Before Judge Crocker
October 26 2003

Judge Crocker, During the buildup to the "Shock and Awe" campaign against Baghdad, and throughout the bombing, and for the first ten days of the occupation of Iraq, I lived in Iraq with Iraqi children and families whom our Voices in the Wilderness campaign had grown to know and love over the course of many visits.

While I was in Baghdad, I saw and heard weapons of mass destruction—sickening thuds, gut-wrenching blasts, horrific explosions. I resolved while there to revisit the U.S. Navy's ELF [Extremely Low Frequency transmitter system] site and assist with offering testimony about the U.S. arsenal of nuclear weapons and its capacity to launch cruise missiles.

The effect of cruise missiles that I saw is negligible when compared to the effect of the Trident nuclear missiles that the ELF system facilitates.

Before the Second Gulf War began, about a dozen of our team members fasted for three days at the Safwan border crossing between Kuwait and Iraq. Facing U.S. soldiers across the border, we at one point spontaneously knelt, praying that the U.S. military would not cross the line. The United States trespassed on the territory of a whole country, crossed the line of an international border in the theory and on the argument that these people might have some weapons of mass destruction that might possibly be delivered to another country. The U.S. launched a so-called "preventive" strike because of missiles that Iraqis might possibly have.

To this date, it's been shown that they didn't have the WMD that they were accused of possessing.

I crossed the line into the Wisconsin ELF facility, here in my own country, to call to the attention of people I live with here that we have Weapons of Mass Destruction. There isn't any doubt that we have them. The government acknowledges that we have them, and the ELF site is the place that can direct the launching of these weapons anywhere in the world, with pinpoint accuracy. These weapons enable a U.S. administration to devise a go-it-alone policy based on threat and force—with these weapons, the U.S. can destroy any country anywhere. They also can destroy us in the process.

The fallout and atmospheric effects can destroy many of us.

If it's wrong for me to sound this alarm, in my own country, without killing anyone, just by walking across the line, then convict me and send me to jail.

Please, go ahead.

That's the logic of our legal and judicial system.

"I would prefer, if you want me to do something useful, that you sentence me to community service and send me to do it in Baghdad. It may even help Mr. Bush because we are Americans and we are trusted by Iraqis who know us. We have a house, we call it Tomorrow House, in a Baghdad neighborhood where we live with no guards and no particular protection. I'd like to return there in mid-December and would faithfully correspond with your court.

Judge Crocker instead sentenced me to a month in Federal prison. Due to bureaucratic error, I haven't served the sentence yet – maybe when they read this I will. The ELF facility was shut down in September, 2004.

I returned to Iraq in August of 2003, to witness more of the Occupation.

All We Want Is Security
September 1, 2003

Since I first met him in 1997, Sa'ad had talked about bringing me to meet his parents and, after he married, his wife and newborn baby.

But fear prohibited the visit. We were nearly certain that Baath party intelligence workers would interrogate Sa'ad almost immediately after a Westerner left his home. Yesterday, John Farrell and I spent the afternoon with Sa'ad and his family. We sat on thin mats in a bare room furnished only with a rickety wooden table and a vase of plastic flowers. The family is fortunate to have a fan and a working telephone.

Sharing the home with Sa'ad are his wife and six-month-old son, Sa'ad's brothers Ra'ad and Qasim, his sister Eman, and his parents. At the doorstep, before we entered, Sa'ad whispered to me that Saddam's *fedayeen* had broken his brother Qasim's nose when they tried to conscript him into military service just before the recent invasion. Because Qasim refused, they tortured him with electric shock.

"This affects him," said Sa'ad, lightly tapping his head. "His mind, it changes."

Sa'ad's older brother Ra'ad, 36, attributes his graying hair to 13 years of military service. Now he works as a taxi driver, but he fears going out on the street because he might be "carjacked." Without an income, he can't support his wife and two daughters who now live with relatives in the countryside.

"All we want is security," Ra'ad emphasized several times during our visit.

There is so much more they could reasonably want. For instance, they served us a meal on a plastic spread they have used with care since 1980. Sa'ad's shirts are clean but have threadbare collars. His mother endures severe arthritis. Under sanctions she couldn't afford medical treatment; she still can't. But the top priority is security.

Today, Abu Wafiq, a father of ten who says he is lucky because no one in his family has been hurt or killed, echoed the need for security. "You can live on one meal a day," he said. "But we need more than food, and first we need security."

Relative security emerges in bizarre ways. Salaam is part of the extended family of Muqtedar Al Sadr, a radical cleric who leads one of the four main factions of the Shi'a faith in Iraq. When the holy shrine of Imam Ali, in Najaf, was recently bombed, killing Sayeed Hakim, analysts wondered if Hakim's followers would exact revenge on the family of Al Sadr. "I am part of this family," said Salaam in a matter-of-fact way. "But the happy news is that twenty members of my family were killed when the shrine was bombed."

It took me several minutes to catch on to the grim reality. No, Salaam is not happy, but since members of his extended family were among those murdered, it's far less likely that opposing factions will turn on his clan.

I haven't yet visited hospitals and clinics in Iraq. Now that U.N. sanctions are lifted, we harbor hopes that at least there we'll find greater security for families seeking to heal their loved ones. Headlines state, however, that the U.N. will drastically reduce its staff by 90 per cent because of insecurity in Iraq.

I don't feel secure here. I feel more uneasy than ever. We venture down streets where armed robbers attack pedestrians in broad daylight. When dusk falls, we anxiously await word that each of our team is safely indoors. At night, sleeping on the roof, gunfire from the street below awakens us. "Keep down," Cathy Breen whispers, as we try to figure out how close the shots are.

One of our team has been mugged and beaten, four have been robbed, one survived the U.N. building bombing, and one was chased down the street at gunpoint.

John Farrell says that the warmth and hospitality he experienced in Sa'ad's home gave him an unusual sense of security. I smiled and asked if he remembered that there was a brief spate of gunfire just outside the home.

On previous trips to Iraq, I felt certain that we had a responsibility to nonviolently resist the sanctions and the impending invasion. It's very hard now to sort out which of the many threats befalling ordinary people here are the most dire. It's difficult to chart a course that will help us voice the cares and concerns of those whom we encounter. Clearly, the situation here requires courage.

In no way do I want to denigrate or dismiss such valid fears. But I in turn have another fear: in the quest for security, people may succumb to the siren song of strong-arm police state tactics. This could mean the revival of Saddam style law and order, complete with informers, goon squads, and other trappings of a reign of terror. As I write, I hear an armored personnel carrier speeding down the street outside. It's followed by the grinding rumble of a tank as the Occupation vehicles travel in tandem. Their presence doesn't make us feel any more secure. These soldiers and people in Baghdad have one thing in common: dread.

A Better World
December 25, 2003

When I was in high school, I participated in a public speaking contest and was asked to present a humorous reading. I chose a passage from the book *The Joyous Season*, in which a young boy describes how his father dreads the Christmas season with the attendant demands to shop and socialize. I still remember the opening line: "Daddy always said that the best place to spend Christmas is in a Moslem country."

Now, having spent several Christmases in Iraq, I'm amazed at how easily one can step into the drama of a light shining in the darkness which the darkness shall not overcome. Several days ago, next door to the home we now rent in Baghdad's Karrada neighborhood, baby Noor was born. Her dark, damp, chilly home resembles a stable. Baby Noor's grandmother begged us for a blanket in which to wrap the newborn. Her aunt, ten-year-old Eman, has no socks and no coat. She smiles as she shivers. Yet Abu Noor and Umm Noor, the proud young parents, are beaming with gratitude and pride as they hold up their newborn. Leaving their home, I realize that they are slightly better off than the family across the street. At least they have a roof overhead.

Our neighbors on the other side of the street are living in a junk-yard, sheltered by flimsy construction. Looking out of our second floor window, Cynthia and I wept with chagrin during this morning's downpour as we watched two young women navigate their way through garbage and mud puddles to collect clothing that had been hung outside. We call our home "the fridge" because, with only two to three hours of electricity during most of the past four days, our electric heaters don't work. It's a sheer act of will to wriggle out of a sleeping bag, cast aside blankets, and face a chilly bathroom and kitchen. Imagine the hardship for those living in tents and shanties.

Whether comfortable or forlorn, military or civilian, everyone in Baghdad is afflicted by the ongoing war. A Kenyan woman, Sylvia, has been emailing me encouraging messages for the past several months. Today she expressed distress over news of mayhem and bombing in Baghdad at Christmastime. "Even in World Wars, Christmas was a time when armies called for a ceasefire," wrote Sylvia. "I wonder if that only applied when both sides were Christian?" The sad irony here is that people in every neighborhood of Baghdad and other Iraqi cities braced themselves for the onset of Christmas and New Year holidays, expecting violence to rise.

As I write, mortar blasts and bombings have been going on for the past hour, and now a siren wails a warning for the Coalition Provisional Authority personnel. I can't imagine where they or anyone else could go for shelter. As our friend Umm Heyder said in Chicago, when we asked her thoughts about the capture of Saddam Hussein, "The whole city is captured."

Koranic and New Testament stories celebrate the journey three kings made, bearing gifts for the newborn Prince of Peace. Better for the rulers of today's world, and for every merchant of death who serves them, to stay *away* from the children.

Yes, the Christmas traditions, ranging from the shepherd's generosity to Herod's persecution, come alive here in Baghdad. The stories, if embraced, could teach us a better way. Peter Maurin, who helped found the Catholic Worker movement, wrote in one of his delightful "easy essays" that, "The world would be better off if people would stop trying to become better off."

I am sure that many people worldwide share my friend Sylvia's deep regret. I hope they are thinking of ways to stop paying for war. Most governments today do not want our bodies on the front lines of combat. They want our assent and our money. I hope millions are marking their calendars for March 20, 2004, and helping to plan demonstrations against the inconclusive war that began on March 20, 2003. And I hope all will feel the warmth and goodness of that light which shines bravely in Umm Noor's gleaming eyes, as she stands barefoot on a cold, cement floor, joyfully cradling her newborn babe.

Rebuilding
January 1, 2004

Oral traditions eventually recorded in the Book of Exodus tell the tales of the ancient Israelites' escape from bondage in Egypt. A cruel Pharaoh was ruthless in his murderous demands. Already crushed by the work of building monuments to their oppressor, they were then ordered to also gather the straw to make the bricks that would be used for building. It was the last straw. The Israelites began to heed revolutionary calls for escape.

Today I visited the former Iraqi Air Defense Camp in Baghdad. Under Saddam Hussein's regime, now legendary for ruthless repression, military officers and their families were given decent housing. In this camp, they even had two swimming pools. Heavily bombed during Operation Shock and Awe, the compound's main buildings are now heaps of rubble, with a few long, gray tubular U.S. missiles scattered on the debris. Following the U.S.-led invasion of Iraq, at least four hundred families moved into this camp. It's one of several similar vacated and bombed areas that have been "squatted" by desperate families who prefer eking out an existence amid the wreckage to whatever misery they left behind.

Before the Occupation, in poor neighborhoods such as the oft-cited Saddam city, renamed Sadr City, several families would inhabit one hovel. I can well imagine the infighting over scarce resources that would inspire a young couple to pick up their meager belongings and move. What's more, when local and absentee landlords realized that there was no government system to prevent them from evicting people and raising the rents, numerous families found themselves kicked out of their homes at gunpoint or unable to pay skyrocketing rents. Under Saddam's regime, landlords would face long-drawn-out court appeals in their efforts to evict people, perhaps because the regime couldn't cope with greater numbers of homeless and displaced people. In spite of appalling conditions, it's clear that the people who are squatting in this camp have gambled on the possibility that enduring present hardships could lead to something better in the future.

The children in the camp are among the loveliest little ones I've ever met. They were shy, but smiling, friendly, and incredibly well behaved. The collapsed buildings and mounds of debris don't seem to faze them. Several of them worked industriously atop hills of rubble, their little hands digging for intact bricks. They bring the bricks to their parents who use them to build new housing walls.

At least a dozen of the children have large red spots covering their faces. It could be that they've been bitten by midges or fleas. But now visitors begin to wonder if they're affected by contaminants from the bomb parts. A proper needs assessment of this new housing area ought to be undertaken right away. Clearly, they will need a new ration distribution system. For now, parents return to the "old neighborhood" to pick up ration distributions, since they have no formal identification as residents in the squatters' camp. The new "householders" need access to clean water, medical care, a clinic, and a school. Yet it seems unlikely that their dismal situation will gain much attention in the near future.

Huddled over candles during the U.S. war to liberate Iraq, while gut-wrenching explosions continued late into the night, my companions and I talked about how we must work in the future, not only to help rebuild Iraq but, even more crucially, to rebuild ourselves, our way of life. We must find a way to share our resources, live more simply, and prevent the U.S. from going to war in order to exploit other people's resources.

The Pentagon system has become the new Pharaoh. Our reliance on threat and force to resolve problems inspires other leaders and cultures to act similarly. The warmongers rob people of the resources needed to build a better world. I think of the little ones digging for bricks, growing up in desperate conditions, and I wonder what sort of revolutions we can expect. The promised land that so many of us learned about as we listened to scripture stories will never be found by electing or following warmongers.

We face a tall agenda. Rebuild Iraq. Rebuild ourselves. And insist on compassion for the little builders in Iraq who may be poisoned by their very efforts to build a sheltering wall.

The Two Troublemakers
December 22, 2004

Last evening, in Amman, we met with Fadi Elayyan and Jihad Tahboub, two Palestinian young men who were imprisoned for two months, without charge, by U.S. occupying forces who seized them in Baghdad on April 10, 2003.

They are trying to help four of their companions who are still held by the U.S. military, presumably in a prison compound at Umm Qasr, in southern Iraq.

"On April 10, the U.S. Marines kidnapped us," Jihad began in a matter-of-fact tone. "We were students, and we stayed in Baghdad during the war because we did not want to give up our studies or leave our friends. The Marines wanted to occupy our building because it is high and gives a good view of the area." Some of the students had Palestinian passports. When they asked what they were guilty of, the soldiers said, "You are guilty of being Palestinian."

"You are not studying education in Baghdad," the soldiers told them. "You are studying terrorism."

"We said that we had citizen IDs and we are students," said Fadi, but the soldiers insisted, with guns pointed at their heads, "You are in Iraq and you are terrorists."

Fadi, aged twenty-four, had been living in Baghdad for six years. At the Mustansariya University, he was three months short of achieving a degree in environmental engineering. Jihad, aged twenty-three, studied hotel management. Fadi and Jihad were released from a prison in Umm Qasr two months later, on June 10, after a U.S. military tribunal issued each of them signed but undated documents stating that there was no evidence to support a claim that he committed a belligerent act against the Coalition forces. Before being released, they had to sign a document stating that the U.S. military bore no responsibility for what had happened to them while they were in custody.

"It was inhuman, the way they treated us," said Fadi. "For the first seven days we were given no food or water." On the first day, they were handcuffed and taken to the Hasan Al Bakr Palace where they stayed overnight on wet ground, outdoors. "We tried to bury ourselves in the sand to keep warmer," Fadi recalled. "All the time they were pointing their guns at us. They made us feel that we are going to die now, they gonna kill us now." The next day they were taken to Saddam Airport where they were again held outside, in the cold, without food. "They were laughing while they were searching us and throwing us on the ground. They took pictures of us which they said they would send back to their families in the U.S."

It was a full month before the International Commission of the Red Cross enabled any contact between the students and their families.

From the Saddam Airport, they were taken to the Imam Ali Air Base at Nassiriyeh, traveling by truck. They stayed there two days, again outdoors. If anyone screamed out, they were beaten, by hand or with rifle butts.

From the Imam Ali Air Base, they were moved to a huge prison compound in Umm Qasr where approximately 10,000 prisoners were held. Civilian prisoners were separated from combatants. At first, they were held in an area which consisted of fifteen compounds, each compound holding around five hundred prisoners. "They give you one blanket, but it's not enough. We did not cover ourselves with the blanket, we used it as a mat," said Fadi.

"There was no place for us to stay in the big tent," he continued, "so we built our own tent by sticks. I asked for a stick from a guard who was outside the fence. He didn't respond, so I asked, 'Why don't you answer me?' He said, 'You are my enemy. I don't have to speak with you.' I asked, 'Who said I am your enemy?' He said, 'If you say one more word, I will kill you.'"

After initial processing in the large compound, they were moved to a second part of the prison called "Bucca," named after a fireman who was killed at the World Trade Center.

"There was a picture of the twin towers in front of the prison," said Jihad, "just to make the soldiers feel they are doing the right thing, just to make them feel it is in the right way."

Fadi and Jihad particularly detested the way their captors treated the children who were imprisoned with them. "There were thirteen-year-old kids in with us," Fadi said. "Sometimes they would throw candies from their humvees, shouting, 'Bark like a dog, and I'll throw you the candy.' Some of the small children were crying in the night, asking to go home to their families. We were trying to get them quiet."

"Some of the prisoners were criminals, thieves. They put the children with them. Some of them tried to abuse children. We told the guards, they started laughing."

"One prisoner tried to rape a kid and he refused, so they made a cut on his face."

Occasionally, Fadi and Jihad would refuse to take their food because of the way soldiers in the "Feeding Team" taunted them. "Say that you love Bush and I will give you food," a soldier would say, before handing them a bowl. "I told them, 'I don't love Bush. I don't love Saddam, I love only myself,'" said Fadi, "but a person has to have some honor." Telling them to keep the food, Fadi added, "Let me go and I will cook my own food."

Fadi and Jihad tried to speak up on behalf of other prisoners. "They called us 'the two troublemakers' because we were the only two that spoke English in the whole compound.

"After seven days, we tried to make our demands more organized. We didn't ask anything about our legal situation because, when we asked them, they said it is not our responsibility, so we started trying to make our living conditions better."

"We were asking for enough food, potable water, water for washing ourselves—skin diseases are contagious one from another. We were asking for more medical support. Many people had to make a dressing change. Many had to take injections. They refused all our demands."

Sensing that some of the soldiers would be aware of Fadi's and Jihad's strength of character, we asked if they ever encountered some sensitivity on the part of the soldiers. "Seldom would you find someone with feeling," was Fadi's response. "Maybe the girls, they would have more feelings than men, but even they kept on laughing when they'd see someone injured or in pain."

"The U.S. soldiers are young, in their twenties, I don't believe that any one of them will feel regret. Most of them were saying, 'If you do any wrong thing I will kill you.' Most of them don't have feelings, any kind of feelings. They just do what they are told to do."

"They don't care," Jihad added. "One soldier was in a truck and she pointed at the American flag and she said, 'This is your flag.'"

When they were finally brought before a tribunal, interrogators asked them if they had any information about weapons of mass destruction or if they knew the whereabouts of Saddam Hussein. The judge at the tribunal, a military officer, determined that they should be released from administrative detention. Soldiers drove them to Basra, the nearest large city, gave them each five dollars, and set them free. Now "the troublemakers" are deeply troubled by the fate of their four companions who are still imprisoned at Umm Qasr, "guilty" of being Palestinians.

A Batch of TCNs
January 15, 2004

"We've given up hope," said twenty-year-old Mohammed Al Katib, a Palestinian student imprisoned in the Umm Qasr prison camp in southern Iraq. "We don't think we'll ever get out of here." On January 3, 2004, I traveled with Rev. Jerry Zawada and several of our Iraqi friends to Umm Qasr, located on the Iraq-Kuwait border. There, in a remote and desolate area where U.S. Coalition authorities have constructed a network of tent prisons, we visited four Palestinian students who've been held for many months by U.S. coalition authorities. In the "Bucca Camp," prisoners and guards alike battle against monotony, anxiety, and isolation. The prisoners we met listed one more emotional pitfall: despair.

We left Baghdad just after sunrise that Saturday morning and drove six hours to Basra, without stopping, hoping that we might reach Umm Qasr before visiting hours ended. At the outskirts of the prison, a U.S. soldier whose badge read MP (Military Police) politely told us that we were too late. Visiting hours lasted from 9:00 a.m. to 1:00 p.m., Thursday to Saturday. The next opportunity to visit would be five days later. Reluctant to leave, we asked if an exception could be made, explaining that we'd come a long way on a difficult stretch of road and that some of us would leave Iraq within the next several days.

The MP, a young dental hygienist from Tennessee, agreed to contact Major Garrity, a woman whom our Christian Peacemaker Team friends in Baghdad assured us would do her best to help. She initially said, "No way, today we already processed a batch of five hundred new prisoners." After some further conversation, she hesitated and then said, "Hang on. Maybe we can do something." I think she knew how beleaguered the young men we hoped to see were feeling and wanted to give them some small measure of hope. An hour later, jostling on the benches of an Army jeep, we were transported over bumpy desert terrain to the prison visitors' tent at Compound 11, Tampa 11, where Officer Lou, formerly a Miami cop, had delivered four men in their early twenties, each of them former students in Baghdad.

Prison authorities refer to the young men as "TCNs," Third Country Nationals. Four of them were arrested in their dorm rooms on April 10, the day after U.S. Marines arrived in Baghdad. When they asked the Marines what crime they had committed, they were told they were guilty of being Palestinians. The students presume that the Marines wanted to occupy their building because it was one of the tallest in the area and offered a good view. A fifth youngster, Ameer Abbas, a Palestinian who has Iraqi citizenship, was on his way home from his university on June 23, 2003, when a shootout erupted at the local mosque. Clutching his textbooks, he ran in the opposite direction. U.S. soldiers spotted him running and arrested him. His brother, a dentist in Baghdad, has tried repeatedly to secure his release. Dr. Amer Abbas accompanied us to the prison, hoping for a second visit with his brother.

Two other students who were arrested at the same time as Jayyab, Mohammed, Basel, and Ahmed were released in June of 2003, perhaps because they spoke English and were better able to plead their case. Since then, they have explored every possible means of helping their companions who remain in prison. Upon hearing that a handful of westerners with Christian Peacemaker Team and Voices in the Wilderness might be able to help, they contacted our small delegation as soon as we arrived in Amman, in late December of 2003. We promised to do our best. In Baghdad, Christian Peacemaker Team members scoured their list of 6,000 prisoners and found the Capture Tag numbers for two of the prisoners. Available details for all five prisoners filled only one sheet of paper.

Guards assured us that prisoners in the Bucca Compound are better off than those who are held in Baghdad prisons. "We give them clothes, they each get a blanket, and we feed them," said a guard. "We try to do everything we can for them." I think the guards feel compassion, but there's little they can do to help these young men. Certainly, no one can do anything about the fact that the students have already lost two years of studies because of missed exams.

Officers in the Bucca camp have recommended release for these prisoners, but the only people with authority to issue releases are the Baghdad based members of the "Sec-Det," the Security Detainees Review Board. A prisoner's best hope for release rests on their paperwork arriving at the desk of the Sec-Det group as part of a "boarding" process. As our hour-long visit came to a close, we promised the five students that we would try our best to bring more attention to their cases by contacting elected representatives in the U.S., foreign embassies, and the International Commission of the Red Cross.

"Can you think of anything else we can do?" I asked, as we bade the youngsters farewell. "Please," Jayyad Ehmedat said firmly, "there are many here. Help us all."

The people we left behind in the Bucca compound were not criminals. Every time I left Iraq, during sanctions, war, and occupation, I felt as if I were leaving one big prison. How ironic that Voices in the Wilderness members were accused of being criminals, while we felt, every time, like we were leaving the scene of a vast crime. But whenever I have been released from U.S. prisons, into comfort and security, I have also felt like I was walking away from a vast crime. These crimes are connected. I see a war that is also going on here at home. When I last entered the U.S. prison system, Jayyad's words easily echoed: "There are many here. Help us all."

PART THREE

Letters from Prison

N DECEMBER OF 1988, WHILE I WAS IN A COUNTY JAIL AWAITING transport to Lexington Federal Correction Institution, I woke myself up very early each morning, before it became too noisy to concentrate, to read Howard Zinn's *People's History of the United States*. I remember being absorbed by the book and particularly heartened by Zinn's conclusion that anchored his hopes to a "changing of the guard." Zinn envisions a time when those who've soldiered for or protected establishment norms will change their minds, have a change of heart.

While I was on my top bunk, scribbling notes to friends, urging them to read or reread Zinn's book, nine Guatemalan migrant workers were brought into the Cass County jail for "processing." They had crossed into the U.S. illegally and had been arrested after authorities found them huddled in a concealed space in the back of a truck. Scotty, the guard on duty, grew increasingly frustrated trying to fill in the processing papers. I was called upon to translate, and though my Spanish was inadequate it seemed worthwhile to intervene in order to give the new prisoners the phone number for an immigration lawyer.

I watched as Scotty tried to elicit, from the men, information about their date of birth, their addresses, and dates of marriage. The information simply wasn't forthcoming. Many of the men seemed bewildered by the questions. Scotty's next task was to fingerprint each of the men, an awkward and humiliating process. After about an hour, Scotty put his head in his hands and said, "I hate my f---in' job." It was a painful moment, but it augured well for change.

Scotty came from a family that had once farmed the land in Harrison County, Missouri, but family farms had rapidly dissolved as he grew up. His best chance to feed his own family seemed to lie in taking on the role of "processing" humans, in this case, farmers from another land.

I think Scotty would have gladly been part of Zinn's "changing of the guard."

The cruelty of prison rests in locking up people who are often already feeling remorse and shame for past actions, and then heaping upon them more reasons to feel badly about themselves and allowing almost no means to improve their situation. Parents separated from their children, feeling that they've screwed up their kids' lives, are often snarled at by counselors and guards who say they should have thought about their loved ones before they started causing trouble. People who've committed crimes, often nonviolent crimes which they honestly regret (mainly related to drug use and drug trade), shouldn't be allowed to continue harming themselves or others through drug trafficking. But why take away every other freedom and why employ other poor people to act as "human zookeepers?"

Who can speak up on behalf of people trapped inside U.S. prisons, including those who are working on the lowest rungs, people like Scotty? I learned a lesson about "speaking up" when I first entered the Cass County jail in Missouri, in 1988.

I quickly realized that the other 12 women in the cell, a dingy area called "the Bullpen," were wincing at the sight of a new prisoner encroaching on the minimal space allotted to them. Most had already been there for many weeks. The Bullpen was meant to be a short-term holding area, but because the jail was so overcrowded, the six bunk beds, exposed toilet, metal table and spray-mist shower with a ripped curtain became housing for at least a dozen women prisoners awaiting transport.

Just prior to beginning my sentence I had been released from the hospital following major surgery after a lung collapse caused by a congenital abnormality.

Friends said that in my prison uniform I could have posed for a Soviet Union poster charging the U.S. with abusing prisoners. The women prisoners glaring at me were seeing a 90 pound woman with pink eye, a runny nose, tangled hair, an obnoxious cough, and a facial rash. Eyeing the top bunk assigned to me, I wondered how I'd heave myself up there without stepping on another woman's bed. And how could I stuff the lumpy mattress I carried into the prison-issue casing when I could barely bend down to tie my shoes? At that point, the most intimidating woman in the Bullpen laughed, rolled her eyes, and said, "I don't know what I did so wrong to be locked up with this white motherf----- with AIDS!" My heart sank.

I managed to get up to the top bunk and, over the next hours, women closest to me were curious and then kindly, asking me how I'd ended up in the Bullpen. We found small ways to be helpful to one another. For instance, I had my "week-at-a-glance" address book with me which included a small map of the U.S. Together, other inmates and I found the various federal prisons to which each of us could be sent.

I started to feel better. Within three days, all of the women treated me with affection, calling me "Missiles" for short. "Missiles," said the woman who had first erupted upon seeing me, "I tried my hardest not to like you, but I just can't help myself—I like you."

Major Nick and Sergeant Roy, the officers responsible for running the Cass County jail, were stingy beyond belief when it came to spending the federal money sent to them as reimbursement for housing federal prisoners awaiting transport. We never had adequate supplies of toilet paper, paper towels, cleaning supplies, or eating utensils. In the two months I spent there, only once was a guard "free" to take us outside for fresh air. Painted battleship gray, with bars on three sides of the enclosure and florescent lights that were never turned off, the Bullpen seemed one of the worst outposts of the U.S. prison system.

One day, a woman came into the cell who had been charged with a DUI, driving under the influence. Her lawyer came to bail her out the next day. As she left, I asked if she could leave behind her newspaper. "Oh honey," she said, "you all shouldn't have to read yesterday's news. I'll get them to send in today's paper." I politely said that we'd rather have the old one because when we ran out of toilet paper we used newspaper. As soon as she was outside, she slapped a lawsuit against the prison for failing to respect human rights.

As soon as Major Nick learned of it, he stormed into the Bullpen. "Which one of you all bitches in this here Bullpen had the nerve to say that we do not GIVE you toilet paper?" he bellowed.

I expected a chorus of angry responses, but instead heard, "Musta' been Missiles. She thinks she's living in some kind of hotel!" I was stunned. I felt like a general leading the charge who looks behind, asking, "Where are the troops?"

Major Nick polled each woman in the cell. "Have you EVER had an experience in this Bullpen where your needs were not met?!" Each woman avowed that Major Nick and Sergeant Roy took good care of them.

When my turn came, I listed the items they didn't supply, told him how awful the slop they fed us had been, complained about the miasmic cloud of cigarette smoke hovering over us, and assured

Major Nick that he shouldn't run a kennel for dogs, much less a place where human beings lived.

Hours later, after a glass of kool-aid was spilled on the metal table and we had no paper towel to clean it up, women began shouting, "Guard! Guard! We need paper towels." No paper towels arrived. A sticky puddle trickled onto the floor. Months later, at the Lexington, Kentucky, maximum-security prison where I served the remainder of my sentence, I asked one of the women to help me understand what had happened that day. She helped me see how much power Major Nick and Sergeant Roy had over each of the women. These jailers could interfere with their chances to get "good time," to see their children before they were transported to a faraway prison, to talk with a lawyer, to meet with a clergy person, to purchase commissary items, or to get a box sent in to them with tube socks and an undershirt. I had plenty of "connections" on the outside and had nothing to lose, with a relatively short (one year) sentence and a statement on record that I wouldn't pay any fines. Of all of us in that cell, I was the most privileged in terms of education and financial security.

This story, for me, has become a metaphor. Who had the biggest responsibility, in the Bullpen, to raise her voice? To whom much is given, much is required. When we witness, first hand, serious abuses of fellow human beings, and when we have a chance to raise our voices and perhaps alleviate their afflictions, how can we keep quiet? In our world, many of us who live in the U.S. are perched, quite by accident, amidst inordinately luxurious surroundings, relative to the rest of the world. We're the luckiest.

Not all peace activists can be part of civil disobedience actions resulting in prison sentences. But for those who can, entering the prisons offers an opportunity to better understand how the once lauded war on poverty has become a war against the poor. When I think about my time spent in prison, I recall a world of imprisoned beauty, and yet most of the women I met landed there because of ugly circumstances which they had tried to escape through drug use, drug sales, or both. Here are some of the stories that educated me.

The Warden's Tour
Pekin Federal Prison Camp
April 18, 2004

Several times, during weekday evenings, students pursuing careers as "correction officers" have peered through the window of our rooms as they tour the compound. Their teacher, an assistant warden at Pekin FCI (Federal Corrections Institution), guides them.

I wonder what students think and say after completing the tour.

I'm surprised at how manageable the room I share with nine other prisoners seems to be, just now. Sunlight floods the 18' x 18' space which contains 6 bunk beds, one single bed, 8 lockers, a wooden table and 4 plastic chairs. It could pass for a dorm at an inexpensive youth hostel. Catholic Worker Houses of Hospitality across the country similarly try to utilize space to shelter as many people as possible. With warmer weather here, some women have replaced olive colored wool blankets with white bedspreads.

This brightens the room. Today is Sunday. Soft snores sound comforting to me, as several women, who worked all week, most earning 12 cents per hour, are "sleeping in" and sleeping soundly.

The Pekin, Illinois Federal Prison Camp (FPC) assigns new prisoners to this space, called "the Bus Stop," until a bed is freed in one of the two "alleys," or corridors. Prisoners who violate a rule are also sent here, as punishment. Four of us are newcomers. Six have been placed here for discipline.

"The Bus Stop is turning into a war zone," one young prisoner observed, earlier today, over breakfast. "Didn't you hear that argument last night?" I'm glad I slept through it.

My friend told me that several women returned from a card game, close to midnight and awakened others by rustling through lockers and slamming doors. An argument erupted, leading to an exasperated threat, by one woman, to "snitch." Squabbles between crowded, anxious prisoners are predictable, and they surely wear on people. But the most remarkable feature of prison life, from my limited experience (I served nine months in a maximum security prison in 1989), is the quiet courage that generally prevails amongst the majority of women prisoners I've met.

The living conditions in prisons may not appear onerous to visitors on guided tours. Decisions to limit possessions, issue clothing, and regulate fixed daily schedules can be justified as sensible measures. Many communities, such as the Catholic Worker Houses of Hospitality, struggle with issues that arise over sharing space, meals, tasks, and house rules. The cruel flaw in the prison system lies in the intent to punish people rather than help them. Women must develop and draw from extraordinary reserves of positive, creative energy to battle against the tedium, the routine, and the enforced idleness that descends on people: "the prison fog," as one former prisoner described it.

Mothers separated from their children face deep grief, often feel intense guilt, and yet try to mother their children from afar. Throughout long days, months and years of imprisonment, women learn to cope with resentment toward those who profit from their incarceration – the judges, prosecutors, prison architects, corporation executives and the paid employees of the prisons.

The illusion of "management" was on display for our wide-eyed student visitors this month. But systems, regulations, routines and carefully designed units mask the futility and stupidity of the U.S. prison-industrial complex. Just a few conversations with prisoners swiftly uncover the chaos and confusion caused by wrongheaded policies, which the student visitors will prepare to enforce.

"I was abused every day of my life, as a child," said one young prisoner. "I felt like the only added thing they could do to me was kill me." She's a talented artist. Almost every day, she sketches and colors portraits and scenery on starched handkerchiefs. Working on the floor, next to the Bus Stop table, she carefully letters "I am the resurrection and the life," next to the visage of Jesus' face, which she has just drawn. She can't leave the Bus Stop for regular prison until she agrees to pay a court-imposed fine. "I'm not going to impose that fine on my relatives," she states, while shading Jesus's cheekbones. "There's nothing these people can do that scares me. I don't care if I spend my whole sentence in the Bus Stop."

Imagine a young woman who recalls suffering abuse almost everyday of her childhood growing up to learn that authorities who never helped her then have now set up a decade of punishment for the beginning of her adult life. Once, she escaped into drug use. A court convicted her of a nonviolent drug-related crime. Now she dreams of becoming a missionary in a far away land.

Some say that the prison system is necessary so that society can isolate abusive people from defenseless victims. That's not true. Abusive people can be separated from victims and helped to cope with their sick behavior without losing every other human freedom. Again, the Catholic Worker Houses of Hospitality come to mind. Working as volunteers, seeking merely the chance to join communities dedicated to the works of mercy and simple living, hundreds of idealistic, kindly people have set up havens for their fellow human beings, aiming to treat them as guests and together form community. At no cost to U.S. taxpayers, these communities have been replicated in many of the neediest sections of urban and rural America. Not only do they make it plausible to envision alternatives to lengthy incarcerations for nonviolent offenders, but they also offer a shining testament to the wrongheaded inadequacy of the U.S. prison system as a means to solve human problems.

Five cottonwood trees grow on the Pekin prison compound, plus several maple and fir trees. Some women prisoners have watched these trees grow since they were seedlings, planted six years ago. The Pekin prison camp doesn't attract many birds, but during early morning hours we hear birdsongs from nearby fields. I'm often reminded of a bird taking flight when I see a woman's spirits soar because of an unexpected compliment or simple, sincere word of appreciation.

Mail call, a particularly intense half-hour, follows the 4:00 p.m. daily count, on weekdays. Women cluster around a plastic mail bin. A guard reads aloud a name on each envelope in the bin and waits for the recipient to say, "Pass it."

"We live for mail call," said a long-term prisoner. "It's our only lifeline to the outside." Pangs of disappointment flash across many faces, as most women walk away empty handed. But that quiet courage returns.

The curious students who participated in the Warden's Tour will learn about managing correctional facilities. They'll learn about security within the prison system. If they were to learn about preventing some of the greatest violence that threatens us, they would be studying ways to abolish the causes of war. They would work to restrain those who manufacture nuclear weapons, those who profit from the sale of alcohol, firearms and tobacco, those who create acid rain and other environmental disasters. Instead, they will be indoctrinated in ways to demean and defeat the quiet resolve that prisoners in places like Pekin muster forth to face the days, weeks, months, and years ahead.

I think the Warden's Tour is too short, too superficial. I wish he and his students would venture inside "the Bus Stop" and stay for just three days. It could save them from participating in an abysmally failed system.

May Day
May 1, 2004

It's Saturday morning, May 1, 2004, and women here at Pekin Federal Prison Camp who watched CNN news feel indignant about the way Iraqi prisoners have been treated by U.S. military guards. "Did you see those pictures?" Ruth asked. "What in the world is going on over there?"

The news coverage they watched had photo-ops from last year's May Day, when President George Bush triumphantly boarded the U.S.S Lincoln to declare "Mission Accomplished," juxtaposed with the recently released photos of U.S. military members apparently enjoying degradation and torture of Iraqi prisoners at Abu Ghraib.

"Where did May Day traditions come from?" I later asked aloud, in the prison library. The librarian, Lori, quickly found an encyclopedia entry detailing various May Day traditions. Several of us laughed about one which holds that the dew on the grass on May 1 holds special qualities for restoring youth. Prison authorities would be mighty surprised if we all started rolling on the grass. "It would be better to celebrate morning dew than to boast about dropping all those bombs over Iraq," said Ruth. "Looks like people there are going to hate us so much, they'd rather kill us than look at us."

Discussion turned to an April 7, 2004, press release that came in yesterday's mail. Issued by the American Federal Government Employees Union, it urges members to lobby against Senate Bill 346, introduced by Senators Carl Levin and Craig Thomas. The bill proposes rescinding federal contracting preferences for Federal Prison Industries (FPI).

The FPI, or UNICOR, was begun in 1934, under President Franklin Roosevelt, as a program to keep prisoners busy and equip them with job skills in preparation for release. It now employs 21,000 prisoners. At Pekin, women manufacture armored plates for U.S. military humvee vehicles and also small cages for immigration authorities to use when picking up children for detention or deportation at U.S. borders. The UNICOR workers earn hourly rates ranging from 23 cents to $1.23. Much of that money goes back into prison-related industry if the prison laborers buy highly-priced commissary items or make regular phone calls which cost 25 cents per minute.

At the Federal Correctional Institute (FCI) medium-high security men's prison adjacent to this camp, and at many other FCIs, the

UNICOR factories operate 24 hours per day, employing three shifts of prison laborers.

The laborers may be learning new skills, but their experience won't guarantee them jobs on "the outside" where they are not allowed to even list UNICOR as a reference. Imagine telling a prospective employer that you have 15 years of experience as a welder, but can't supply a reference... and you're an ex-con.

I don't think the American Federal Government Employees Union cares, primarily, about helping prisoners "while away the hours" or prepare for employment after being released. A clue about their interests in maintaining UNICOR lies in the fact that the only ones who can hold a share in UNICOR profits are federal employees. Since the FPI/UNICOR doesn't have to compete with any other industry to procure federal contracts, they can charge any price they want for the products or services they supply. One prisoner here is helping make chains for light switches at her UNICOR job. Each chain sells for $32.

UNICOR factories use antiquated equipment, have a hard time meeting deadlines, and aren't subject to much quality control. If they were forced to be competitive with outside industries, many within the prison system forecast that UNICOR wouldn't last long. However, under the present conditions, UNICOR is a profitable company. The wages are sweat-shop low, the client base (the U.S. federal government) is guaranteed, and there's no need to worry about paying company insurance, retirement benefits, or vacation pay. Nor is the FPI/UNICOR subject to compliance with OSHA regulations.

"Prisoners are responsible for producing a diverse range of products," stated Senator Craig Thomas, a Republican from Wyoming before the Senate Committee on Governmental Affairs, on April 7, 2004, "ranging from office furniture to clothing, from electronics to eyewear, from military gear to call centers and laundry services, to mapping and engineering drafting."

"It is ironic," Senator Thomas continued, "that in recent months as we have been debating the issue of off-shoring of American jobs, we continue to lose good paying American jobs to a government sponsored prison labor program."

In a *Harper's* article from October 2003 Ian Urbina reports that "FPI, the federal government's 39th largest contractor, sells more than $400 million worth of products to the U.S. military." Prison laundries clean, press and repair uniforms. Prisoners manufacture helmets, shorts, underwear, flak jackets and ammunition.

On May Day, 2003, when President Bush proudly outfitted himself in military clothing, posing for a photo-op to proclaim "Mission Accomplished," did he wear clothing manufactured by forced laborers in U.S. prisons?

This May, remembering the "Mission Accomplished" banner displayed behind President Bush a year ago, we need to ask ourselves very carefully, while listening to the stories of prisoners here and abroad, what is the mission? What has been accomplished?

Change Agents
May 19, 2004

"Another world is not only possible, she is on her way. On a quiet day, I can hear her breathing."—Arundhati Roy, Porto Alegre, Brazil, World Social Forum, January 27, 2003

"Kathleen Kelly, report to Admin."

I was routinely cleaning toilets in my dorm at Pekin Federal Prison Camp when the loudspeaker summoned me to the Administration Building. "You're going next door," said the guard on duty. "Someone wants to talk with you."

During a five-minute ride to the adjacent medium-security men's prison, I quickly organized some thoughts about civil disobedience and prison terms, expecting to meet a journalist. Instead, two well-dressed men stood to greet me and then flashed their FBI badges. They had driven to Pekin from Chicago, where they work for the FBI's National Security Service.

Both men were congenial. They assured me that their visit had nothing to do with Voices in the Wilderness violations of federal law in numerous trips to Iraq, where we regularly delivered medicines and medical relief supplies. Nor had they come to talk about why I'm currently imprisoned for protesting the U.S. Army's military combat training school in Fort Benning, Georgia. What they proposed was "a conversation," since they had information which they felt would "help me" and Voices teams in Iraq, both now and in the future. Likewise, I could "help them," and perhaps improve national security, by answering some of their questions.

I said I'd prefer not to talk with them without a lawyer present. The more talkative agent quickly nodded and suggested a follow-up visit with a lawyer. He spoke further about his favorable impressions of Voices in the Wilderness and how useful it would be for our travelers to better understand some of the people whom the Iraqi government, under Saddam Hussein, had assigned to work with us as "minders" during our past trips. He said he had information about "bad things" they had done or had planned to do. Having this conversation would benefit Voices in its travel to other countries as well (Voices has focused solely on Iraq, although some of us have visited other countries with other groups).

At that point, I decided not to talk with them at all. "I don't want to accuse either of you of any wrongdoing," I said, wanting to be polite, "but your organization has used methods that I don't support, and sometimes your job requires you to lie."

Still amiable and interested in some kind of conversation, albeit one-sided, they let me know that they had carefully read our website, www.vitw.org. "We saw the pictures of the children," said the less talkative agent. The three of us were silent for a moment.

His partner mentioned that they've already met with numerous Iraqi Americans, none of whom had anything bad to say about Voices in the Wilderness.

"Do you have any questions for us?" they asked several times. "Is there anything you want to say?"

"Well, yes," I said, finally. "I do want to say something. I don't mean this disrespectfully, but I do encourage you to resign." Smiling broadly, they told me they'd placed a bet about whether or not I'd talk to them, but hadn't anticipated being asked to resign.

"Sorry, my wife wouldn't like it," said one. "I've got a pension to collect," said the other.

Several times, they advised me not to publicize their visit. "You know the Arab mind," one advised. "If you tell people we visited you in prison, they'll never believe you didn't talk with us, and you won't be trusted when you go to other countries." There's no such thing as a monolithic Arab point of view, and what intelligence agencies have done to undermine trust in Iraq and the surrounding region is a chapter unto itself, but I bit my tongue.

I think these men came to see me because they were responding to inquiries from their colleagues in Iraq. Perhaps someone, whom I've known, in Iraq, is being "vetted" for a position within the U.S. Occupation, or perhaps an Iraqi under investigation for wrongdoing named me as one who could vouch for his or her decency. I don't see how I could tell anything about my personal experience that would have been harmful to another person, and maybe I could have been helpful in showing that someone I know was genuinely concerned for innocent civilians.

I'm ambivalent—maybe I should have talked with them. But mainly I feel sad, a bit weary, and somehow responsible because the most crucial "information" Voices in the Wilderness can and should offer seldom reaches the general public, much less officialdom. We tried hard to inform people that hundreds of thousands of Iraqi children died as a direct result of economic sanctions. But it was as though we were part of a defective Jeopardy quiz game. We had answers to questions that would never be asked.

The agents who visited me asked about "bad apples" in Iraq. On Capitol Hill, panels of civilians and military leaders want to punish the few "bad apples" responsible for torture and abuse of Iraqi prisoners. When we clamor for closure of the military combat training school in Fort Benning, a school whose graduates have massacred, tortured, assassinated and disappeared many thousands of people in Latin America, public relations spokespeople for the base say that we are over-reacting to "a few bad apples."

Suppose we set aside the bushels of "bad apples." Military, prison and intelligence gathering structures routinely and inherently involve dehumanizing actions (my encounter with the FBI was, I think, exceptionally benign). Instead of searching for blameworthy bad apples as though we are blindfolded children trying to pin the tail on the donkey, why not carefully acknowledge our collective, passive responsibility for systems predicated on threat, force, and violence. When money, talent, and resources are poured into military systems and prison systems, while health, education and welfare systems compete for inadequate budget allotments, we can expect constant warfare abroad and the quadrupling of prisoner populations at home which has occurred in the U.S. over the last 25 years.

Military and prison structures don't train recruits to view "the enemy" or "the inmate" as precious and valuable humans deserving forgiveness, mercy, and respect, even if they have trespassed against us. These systems don't foster the notion that we ourselves could be mistaken, that we might seek forgiveness, or that we might, together with presumed outcasts, create a better world. Look to Scriptures for such views—they're there—but don't expect love of enemy and the Golden Rule to guide military, prison or intelligence systems anywhere in the world.

U.S. history abounds with remarkable achievements and noble endeavors—the movements to abolish slavery, attain women's suffrage, build unions and establish civil rights, to name but a few. But no country can ever achieve political maturity without willingly looking into the mirror and acknowledging all of its history. The U.S. must come to grips with having been, since World War II (when under the shadow of the mushroom cloud we ushered the world into the nuclear age), a nation constantly at war: Korea, Vietnam, Nicaragua, El Salvador, Grenada, Panama, the first Gulf War, Kosovo, Colombia, Afghanistan, the ongoing war in Iraq. We've waged hot war after hot war, and undergirding all these wars is the continuing war of western economies against the biodiversity of our planet. To preserve our pleasures and privileges, we become the most dangerous, warlike culture in human history.

A few bad apples? Not a chance.

As more pictures of beleaguered Iraqi prisoners emerge, prolonging and swelling a horrid scandal, I can't help but wonder why the images of suffering Iraqi children never raised equivalent concern or indignation in the U.S. or elsewhere in the world.

I won't forget that one of the FBI agents mentioned seeing pictures of Iraqi children on the Voices in the Wilderness website. I'm grateful to him for remembering them. I feel haunted by the infants, the toddlers, the young teens and their heartbroken mothers and fathers whom we met at bedside after bedside in Iraqi hospitals. Walking on the oval track, here in prison, I whisper the names and recall the sweet faces of the little ones I grew to know, fleetingly. All of them were condemned to death. None of them were bad apples. They were precious fruits of loving families. Hundreds of thousands died, some after many days writhing in agony on bloodstained mats, without pain relievers. Some died quickly, wasted by water-borne diseases; as the juices ran out of their bodies, they appeared like withered, spoiled fruits. But no, they weren't bad apples. They could have lived, certainly should have lived, laughed and danced, and run and played, but somehow—honestly, I don't understand it—somehow they were sacrificed, brutally and lethally punished.

Their pictures, each of their stories, had something to say to us. If people in the U.S. had seen their images, day after day, the economic sanctions would never have lasted long enough to claim the lives of over a half million children under age five. These Iraqi children, who couldn't survive abysmally failed foreign policies, still have something to say to us.

"Please call me by all my names," wrote Thich Nhat Hanh, a monk and poet who led the Buddhist non-aligned movement during the Vietnam War. He wants us to fully understand who we are.

We have an extraordinary challenge now, in the wake of the Abu Ghraib prison scandal. Clearly, most people in the U.S. don't want to be aligned with or represented by disgraceful and bullying behavior. But we must resist being misled by finger pointing at "a few bad apples." We should acknowledge that all of us are called upon to be change agents, by changing our over-consumptive and wasteful lifestyles. We must look for every sign of a "climate change" that will help us overcome our unfortunate addiction to war making.

This may be a pivotal time. Consider the early stages of the Civil Rights movement. Participants must have wondered how many beatings, how many lynchings, how many Jim Crow indignities would be heaped on communities before opponents of civil rights would say they were tired of being the bully. In that movement, a pivotal point was reached when Bull Connor ordered police to train fire hoses on peaceful protesters, including children. Frustrated onlookers around the world were horrified. And increasing numbers of U.S. people no longer wanted to be identified with Bull Connor and all that he represented.

"Injustice must be exposed to the light of human conscience," said the Rev. Dr. Martin Luther King Jr., "and to the air of national opinion before it can be cured."

I feel sure that numerous members of the armed services, the intelligence agencies, and various other federal government bureaus, including the Bureau of Prison employees, understand very well why we need radical change in the U.S. I feel sure that an era of reform and a climate conducive to progressive humanitarian measures will recycle into our history.

But all of us need to take advantage of our own opportunities to be agents of change. For some, it may mean walking away from cruel, wrongful, or dishonest work. For others, it may mean becoming whistle-blowers. Still others can announce the truth as they see it in spite of risks to their pensions or job security. When we're willing to call ourselves by all of our names, change can happen.

Change is coming. Light as the breath of excruciatingly beautiful Iraqi children nearing their deaths, demanding as the imploring eyes of their mothers who asked us why...you can feel it coming.

Requiems
June 4, 2004

I've always liked the restful quiet of an empty classroom. Maybe this is why the large room where we wait to start mealtime duties, here at Pekin Federal Prison, feels comfortably familiar. During breaks, I've spent many hours in the dining area reading, writing, studying Arabic, and staring out the window.

Today, looking out the window, I watched Kim LaGore crossing the compound, flanked by Ruth and Malika.

Yesterday, when I left the dish room, I sensed something was terribly wrong. Clusters of women were gathered, many already puffy-eyed and tearful. "It's Kim," I was told. "Her other son just died."

On March 21, 2004, Kim LaGore's younger son, Dustin, was killed in Iraq. He was a 19-year-old U.S. soldier who had tried his best to stay out of combat. Seventy-two days later, Sean, Kim's older son, age 29, died from complications following back surgery. Ruth and Malika, who also lost children while in prison, have been like guardian angels for Kim, holding and helping her through this wretched grief.

Every person in the prison camp yearns to spin a protective cocoon around Kim. The authorities couldn't do much. The system traps their compassion, too. They allowed Kim extra phone calls and submitted a furlough request. I feel sure that they each wished for swift procedures to re-sentence Kim to home confinement during the remaining three months of her sentence. Who wouldn't want to respond humanely to a woman who has lost both of her children within three months time while forcibly separated from her relatives and her hometown community? But the system's wheels turn slowly, very slowly.

"I know many of you don't know what to say," Kim wrote on a card posted in the laundry room of our dorm. Thanking us for surrounding her with kindness, she added, "To be honest, I don't know what to say either, except that we'll make it through…"

I remember my first conversation with Kim, about three weeks after Dustin was killed. Having learned that I had been in Iraq many times and lived there during the "Shock and Awe" campaign, she came to me with his picture and an article she'd written reflecting her pain and confusion. She still has not been able to learn any details about Dustin's death other than that, after two weeks in Samarra, a city north of Baghdad, he was killed in a training accident. "I want to go with you to Iraq," said Kim. "I want to tell Iraqi parents that my son Dustin never wanted to hurt anyone. He never wanted to kill."

Kim is here for a "paper crime". A first time offender, she was convicted of a nonviolent and "victimless" crime. In her former job as a bail bondswoman, she had been anxious that a particular client might not return for a court date, and she insisted that he pay her in cash if she posted bond for him. A prosecutor then accused her of accepting drug money, and Kim was convicted of money laundering. Kim believed she wasn't responsible to determine how her client had raised the money.

Enron, Halliburton, Boeing and Dow Chemical CEOs adeptly cover and shield themselves from harm when accused of shady dealings. I haven't kept informed about their most recent appearances in courts, but I don't want any of them to go to jail. I do want the court of public opinion to regard peddling weapons, designing massive machines for destruction, ravaging the world's ecosystems, and poisoning our environment as criminal behavior. Would these CEOs ever refuse clients who declare foreign wars to exploit other people's resources? Would they ever insist that their clients stop making war against the biodiversity of Mother Earth? What would their thoughts be if they heard Kim's story?

June 26, 2004, is Prisoner Awareness Day in the U.S. We've thought of inviting our network of friends outside the prison to observe the day by making advance agreements to completely suspend all communications with loved ones, friends, and household members for just one day. No phone calls, emails, visits, or conversations. At the end of the day, participants could write about the experience to elected representatives or local media, voicing concern over the isolating and long sentences imposed on U.S. prisoners. The action could give a brief glimpse into the dark frustrations felt by women and men whose contact with loved ones hangs on the slimmest and most fragile of threads. Our society desperately needs the social imagining that could envision alternatives.

But for now, Kim's own words and the wordless comfort brought to her by her fellow "criminals" hold enough for a long lesson. Who are the criminals? What are the most serious crimes? And what happens when compassion dies?

In the Wilderness
June 10, 2004

"It's going to get worse before it gets better," said the Pekin Federal Prison Camp administrator, commenting about overcrowding. "We have about 40 more transports in the pipeline." To alleviate overcrowding, the administrator asked 12 women to voluntarily relocate to Victorville, California, where an FPC is being enlarged to handle more prisoners.

Only women facing three or more years of imprisonment are eligible.

Yesterday, three women stuffed belongings they're allowed to take with them into white net laundry bags, gave final goodbye hugs to friends here, and headed out to California where they will help build a larger prison.

Most of the dozen women who volunteered for relocation to Victorville did so because it will place them closer to their children. "I just hope I can see my kids," said Ana, a young mother whose children live in Arizona. "It's been too expensive for them to come here. I really need to see my kids. I think about them all the time, and it's so hard to cope with being away so long. That's why I'm out on the track running so much. I just try to run and pray."

Shortly after I arrived here, Ana supplied me with used but quite usable gym shoes, a tote bag, and sweatpants. Several other women recalled her kindness and joined me in hoping she'll be similarly welcomed in Victorville.

I had presumed that the Bureau of Prisons would use "Con Air" or a prison bus to take women to Victorville. Remembering prison air and bus travel 15 years ago, I still shudder. In a weeklong trip, zigzagging all over the country, we were locked up in different county jails each night. Our wrists and ankles were shackled as we boarded; on the tarmac, armed guards with their guns raised encircled the planes. Prisoners often arrive at their destination sleep-deprived, hungry, disoriented, and scared.

What a relief, then, to know that furloughs were granted for Ana and the others who have set out in groups of three over the past several weeks. Each woman is given $50 and a bus ticket. But, hang on. If these women can be trusted to travel cross-country, carrying cash, on a public bus, and if they're trusted to turn up for self-surrender at a federal prison, why can't they be paroled to home confinement and probation? Why can't U.S. taxpayers be relieved of expenses to imprison them and, in many cases, to provide guardian-ship for their children?

Deneise, who lives in the cubicle next to me, works as the librari-an during several evening and weekend shifts. She also teaches yoga, helps coordinate photo opportunities for women in the visiting room, shares her expertise in ceramics, and sings in the gospel choir. "You with your 13 jobs," joked one friend, "how is anyone ever supposed to find five minutes to talk with you?" I smiled, knowing she barely gets five minutes to herself on many days as a steady stream of women find her, seeking advice, a favor, or a word of comfort. Prisoners and guards alike share regard for Deneise.

One Sunday evening, in the library, just before closing time, Deneise asked if I had time to watch a seven-minute video. "It's my favorite possession here," she said. "We made it the night before I self-surrendered." Filmed in her hometown chapel, the video shows her seven-year-old son, Joshua, delivering Martin Luther King's "I Have A Dream" speech. The child's fine diction and timing, plus his obvious appreciation for the words he'd memorized, evoked pride and affec-tion in the audience. When his voice rose at the end of the speech, promising freedom, the congregation erupted in applause that must have infused the youngster with pride and hope.

"Deneise," I asked, "was that Joshua with you, earlier today, in the visiting room?"

"Yes," she said softly, "that was my Joshua." Now a 12-year-old boy, he was resting his head on her shoulder as his plump arm encircled her waist. Joshua will be 25 when Deneise is released. She was con-victed of money laundering and sentenced to 18.5 years.

"Connie cried herself to sleep last night," said Ruth. "I was praying for her at midnight, and she was still crying." Connie has been here for five years and has nine more to go. All of the new prisoners know her because she helps to lead an orientation designed to help new-comers adjust. Connie presents a session about "long-termers" and "short-termers." Over half of the women here face eight or more years in prison. 82 per cent are first time nonviolent "offenders"; virtually everyone hopes for new laws that would allow for early release. "Don't get your hopes up, and don't call your family with rumors about everybody getting out. You set yourselves up for disappoint-ment that way," Connie counseled, "and you don't want to do that to your kids." But even Connie had begun to think the combination of budget cuts and prison overcrowding might offer some hope. It's a setback to learn that the BOP will cope by enlarging and opening new prisons. Connie's two sons are a foot taller each time she sees them. The younger boy, a high-schooler, vows that he'll enroll in a university near Pekin so that he can be closer to his mom. A petite athlete, Connie is a pillar of nerve and strength here. "Bad days happen," said Carol, another long-termer. "Happens to all of us."

"Connie was so down last night," said Ruth, "that she said might as well volunteer for Victorville and move out of her sons' lives, make it easier for them, let them go on without trying to include her. She says she's not really part of what's going on in their lives now anyway." Ruth, Carol and others saw Connie through the hard slump. Her spirits revived after a few days.

Thinking of women headed to California in hopes of keeping their families together while enduring long prison sentences, I dipped into John Steinbeck's novel, *The Grapes of Wrath*. In the wrenching tale of migrant families, called "Okies," who headed toward California in search of food, shelter and work, Tom Joad, a main character, kills a man in self-defense. Tom had become involved with a preacher, Casy, who tried to convince the migrant families to band together when greedy landowners cheated and abused them. The landowners hire paramilitaries to hunt Casy down and kill him, in retaliation for organizing a labor strike. The thuggish guards go after Tom Joad next. He suffers a severe blow to his head, then attacks his assailant and flees, unsure whether or not he murdered the man. Realizing that he's now a liability to his family, Tom hides out. Only his mother knows where he is. Every day she drops off food for him. One evening, Ma Joad waits for him to fetch the meal. Warning him that he's no longer safe in his wilderness hideout, she urges him to disappear into a big city.

Tom has been thinking about Casy, the preacher.

> "We talked a lot" said Tom. "Used to bother me. But now I been thinkin' what he said, an' I can remember all of it. Says one time he went out in the wilderness to find his own soul, an' he foun' he didn' have no soul that was his'n. Says he foun' he jus' got a little piece of a great big soul. Says a wilderness ain't no good, cause his little piece of a soul wasn't no good 'less it was with the rest, an' was whole. Funny how I remember. Didn' think I was even listenin'. But I know now a fella ain't no good alone." (*The Grapes of Wrath*, Chapter 28).

Ma Joad didn't want her family to "crack up," but ultimately she learns that her family is strongest when they can share their meager resources, even with strangers. And she must find courage to accept her beloved son's self-sacrifice on behalf of others.

Within U.S. prisons, a host of contemporary Ma Joad and Tom Joad protagonists passionately appreciate family values and yearn for ways to strengthen the fabric of society by embracing needy people. The absurdly long sentences imposed on hundreds of thousands of the 2 million people imprisoned in the U.S. are every bit as dehumanizing and cruel as the measures taken against migrant workers who were and still are often regarded as less than human.

I find some comfort in knowing that English literature teachers and students explore themes in *The Grapes of Wrath* in classrooms coast to coast. If they need to draw comparisons with comparable hero figures desperate to nurture families and community in the midst of calamity and loss, I'd recommend Ana, Deneise, Connie and trios of women prisoners heading to Victorville, dying to see their kids.

Lupe
June 30, 2004

"Two days an' a wake-up, Ms. Kelly," sings a prisoner as my out date approaches. In 90 days at Pekin Federal Prison Camp I've spun through a revolving door compared with realities experienced by most of the 2.1 million inmates currently housed in U.S. prisons.

A friend sent me an inscription carved over the entrance of a Polish prison. "When you enter here," it reads, "do not despair. When you leave here, do not rejoice."

I shared this quote with my co-defendant, Cynthia Brinkman, whom the whole compound calls "My Nun." ("Where's my nun?" someone yells. "I need a prayer." "She's not your nun," another argues. "She's MY nun!") Cynthia read the inscription, gave me a knowing look, and said, "You're rejoicing."

She's right. I'm ready to leave, and perhaps I've had one foot out the door during much of my time here. But I'm also subdued by the realization that by any rational assessment I shouldn't be the next one out the door, not when many mothers incarcerated with me haven't seen their children in years. Lupe, for instance.

Yesterday, Lupe was thrilled because I gave her my "TV Day," which meant uninterrupted access to three hours of Hispanic "soaps." Later that same afternoon, Lupe came to see me while I was doing laundry. "Look, Kathy, I brought my gang to come and thank you."

The "Gang" is the sweetest trio of young mothers imaginable. "Are you going to write about us before you go?" asked Lupe, as she and her friends helped me fold laundry. "C'mon, ask me questions."

Q and A with Lupe brought nervous giggles, tears, and a rush of memories. "They don't treat you like a person. You're just a number to them," she said, recalling her court date in Indianapolis three years ago, when a judge sentenced her to nine years in prison on drug charges. Her supporters had filled the courtroom. Among them was her grandfather, who had traveled all the way from Mexico for the trial. Many people had written letters asserting that Lupe was indeed a good girl, that she had never gotten in trouble before. "The tough girls, they used to beat me up," said Lupe, laughing, "because I didn't do bad things." It wasn't until she met and later married her boyfriend that she became involved with drugs. "But the lawyers, the judge, they don't care about your past life. My public defender didn't try to help me. He never told me what was going on. I didn't know what to say or do. And the judge made fun of all the people who came to the sentencing hearing. He said I'd need them more while I was in prison than while we sat in his court."

Now, with her daughters, Alexandra, aged 5 1/2, and Lizette, 4, living in Mexico, Lupe does need help. She needs someone to bring them to Pekin for a visit. "I miss my daughters so much," lamented Lupe, who hasn't seen her girls since July 2001. "It's driving me crazy."

Each 15-minute phone call to Mexico costs $8.35. Lupe works hard to earn enough to manage a weekly call. Even though she is the main orderly for our unit, her wages, which have risen from 12 to 20 cents an hour during her confinement, are barely enough to cover this one brief conversation. "I call every Monday, at 1 p.m. Sometimes they forget to have my daughters there," said Lupe, referring to her in-laws, who are now raising the girls. (Lupe's husband is himself serving a 27-year sentence.) "I can understand; they're getting bigger now, doing things. Still, it hurts. I live for that phone call." The pain in her voice is all too evident. "The other thing that hurts bad—my younger daughter, she doesn't want to talk to me. The older one says, 'Mommy, Lizette doesn't love you, but I do.' And the older one says, 'Mommy, I don't want you to be in prison any more; I want you to come home.'"

Each day, Lupe walks between four and six miles on the oval track. "That's where you can go to think a little more, and to cry," she says. "I think about what I'll do when I get out. Everything will be for my daughters. I can't wait to take them to the Brookfield Zoo, and to the Mexican Day parade."

"There are so many things I think about. What would it be like to fix their hair, to take them to the park, to make meals for them? I don't even know my daughters' favorite colors. I know Alexandra's favorite song." Tears spilled down Lupe's cheeks. "Twinkle, Twinkle, Little Star."

"When I get out, I'll think three times before I do anything. I'll ask myself how it will affect my daughters, our future. Will it help them grow up strong? I want them to grow up strong, not weak, like me."

I asked Lupe if she really believed she was weak. She flashed her brilliant smile, dark eyes still filled with tears. "No," she said. "I'm strong."

Cynthia and the others whom I left behind at Pekin FPC carefully monitor the daily news, looking for updates about legislation that would revive systems of parole for federal inmates. Prisoners across the U.S. are also keenly interested in a proposal being considered by the American Bar Association to abolish mandatory minimum sentencing.

"Kathy, tell me the truth," said Lupe. "Do you think there's a chance I could go home before my time is up?" I've no idea, but I promised Lupe I would join efforts to reform a system that condemns first time offenders charged with nonviolent crimes to harsh mandatory minimum sentences. As it stands now, Lupe must wait 53 months before she'll hear "two days an' a wake-up."

The Bad Sisters
1989, Lexington FCI

As stated above, whether in minimum or maximum security federal prisons, I've yet to meet "the bad sisters." Here are profiles of the women I was closest to in maximum security prison in 1989. The most emotionally trying experience for me, during that stretch, happened the night before I was to be released. Prisoners celebrated my good fortune with an outdoor party, after which I hid in the laundry room, near hysterics, and broke down. I felt like someone who had witnessed a hit-and-run car accident and feared I would walk away without doing anything to help.

Ne-Se

"What you see me doing right now is what you always gonna see me doing... NOTHING! I'm not Hazel, and I sure ain't Aunt Jemima!"

Ne-Se's voice fills the empty dining halls as Anna and I tidy up after the breakfast meal. We count on Ne-Se to keep us going through what would be a very long morning.

Anna and I marvel at Ne-Se's ability to judge what might land her in segregation and how far she can push authorities here. She seems to have a sixth sense in that regard. She's spent two years in "the system" unscathed by incident reports or "shots." Many of the officers can't help but appreciate her comic talent, even when they themselves are the butt of her sarcasm. Warm brown skin, large eyes, high cheekbones, and a regal bearing render this 35-year old woman a striking, dynamic presence.

Brandishing a hand towel, Ne-Se shifts to an authoritative tone. For emphasis, she uses a preacher's exaggerated drawl. "I will come to whatever place they assign me. I'll bring my body here, and you MIGHT see me working' one hour out of every eight hours, but I AIN'T working any eight hours. NO! I'm not the one!" Her eyes flash around the Dining Hall as the wave of defiance crests; then she resumes matter-of-fact reasonableness. "They don't pay you a goddam thing...when I gets OUT, I'm gonna work. Uh—huh. I'll even work for minimum wage, but I'm NOT gonna work here. They didn't send me here to work. I'm here for punishment. I HAD me a job on the outside."

"Selling drugs!" a co-worker calls out as she passes our dining hall. We laugh, but Ne-Se quickly assumes mock seriousness. "Now I gots my diploma, you can't expect me to DO the same work. Do a doctor do the same work as an intern?"

Ne-Se's diploma refers to successful completion of the Adult Basic Education Test, indicating 8th grade level skills. Rumor has it that the answers were for sale, but with or without competence to pass the ABE test, Ne-Se's intelligence is clearly evident. She's quick-witted, shrewd, and able to express her analyses of situations in side-splittingly funny street talk. Recently, when she was asked to take a routine urine test, she resented an intrusive guard's questions about her medical history. Ne-Se put him in his place with haughty truthfulness. "You a piss collector. You just supposed to stand there and collect piss."

Quick to spot inefficiencies and indecencies in the system, she readily voices indignance on behalf of others. One morning we were all exclaiming over the murky, greenish color of the scrambled eggs being prepared for the hospital and segregation units. Ne-Se spied a Food Service director approaching and boomed forth "WHO gonna eat them ROTTEN eggs?!" The foreman supervising food preparation fixed her with a stare that bordered on rage, but the eggs were quickly disposed of. Ne-Se continued her oration as we proceeded down the hall, still within earshot of the Food Service director. "Kelly, they had no business putting those eggs on the line in the first place, and whoever put 'em on the line shoulda been sent to segregation and made to eat 'em ALL."

Ne-Se's outspokenness often extends on the behalf of women who are put down by other inmates. I've watched her step in where angels fear to tread. One day, Pumpkin, a tough, loud woman whose whims generally went unchallenged, was mocking a very nervous, new worker, a woman in her fifties. Seeing the older woman, Marie, grow teary-eyed with mortification, Ne-Se intervened and suggested that Marie and Ne-Se trade places because Pumpkin sure as hell wasn't going to push Ne-Se around. A loud argument ensued which Ne-Se eventually ended by lowering her voice and simply repeating softly "O.K., Chop, you just have a good day. I hope you have a good day." Ne-Se calmly sought out Marie, who had taken refuge in our dining hall. She embraced Marie, let her cry for a while, and assured her that she didn't have to take any guff from anyone.

In spite of her advanced capacity for rebellion, Ne-Se is convinced that she needed to come to a prison like Lexington FCI. "Kelly, I was a hazard to society and a hazard to myself." I wonder if there could have been alternatives to prison. Her experience as a heroin addict grew sordid in the years leading up to her eventual arrest. She was resorting to prostitution to attain drugs, bringing strangers into the house, and upsetting her children. Ne-Se's body bears the scars of drug use; she's particularly distressed by her hands which remain so swollen that it's difficult to detect her knuckles. While Ne-Se can accept punishment as means of negative reinforcement, ("I HATES this place and I never want to come back to it"), she is bewildered by the government's readiness to harm her children by sending her so far away from them. "That hurts more than anything—the separation from your children. Why they have to send you so far? I'm not just talking about women who have children, cause there are women who have children but aren't really mothers because they don't care about their kids. I'm talking about MOTHERS who need and want to care for their kids."

Ne-Se has three children, Gina, 18, Martin, 16, and 'Lil Bit' (Mischa), 12. Like many women here, Ne-Se finds motherhood an intensely sensitive subject, riddled with layers of defensiveness, guilt, confusion, and sorrow, but also tapping her resources of fierce protectiveness and joyful love. The first day I met Ne-Se, I recall her glowering at a group of co-workers having a raucous discussion about sex. "Hmmmph!" Ne-Se sighed impatiently. "They all the time talking about how the first thing they gonna do when they gets out is find theyself a man. Not me. First thing I'm gonna do is hug my daughter. " A delighted smile broke across Ne-Se's face. She rocked back and forth with her arms wrapped around the imagined child. "Uh-huh, I'll hold her, and she cry and I cry. She my world to me. She my sex."

Some weeks later, Ne-Se asked me for help writing a letter to the parole board. "Kelly, I want them to understand that I'm in an emergency situation." When Ne-Se was first arrested, her children moved in with her mother, whom Ne-Se describes as an extremely strong and stern woman. Several months later, Ne-Se learned that 'Lil Bit,' 11 years old at the time, was pregnant. Ne-Se's mother, a bishop of a church strongly opposed to abortion, refused to consider termination of her granddaughter's pregnancy. "If I was out on the street, I can promise you one thing," Ne-Se says firmly. "Lil Bit would not have had that baby." 'Lil Bit' refuses to name the father, perhaps fearing for the man's safety in the light of Ne-Se's wrath. "I'll find out who done it," Ne-Se vows with grim determination.

Ne-Se's letters to the parole board emphasize how urgent it is for her to return to her children and to help her youngest daughter care for the newborn infant. She lays out a parole plan which includes employment at Pete's Tomato Packing Company, a stable residence with her mother, initially, in the Washington D.C. area, and plans to pursue education and possibly complete the apprenticeship in welding which she began several years ago.

Her persistent letters haven't been in vain. She was sentenced to ten years for the crime of having conspired to distribute cocaine, but the judge recognized Ne-Se was selling to support a habit and so sentenced her under a special program for drug abusers. She was given a reduced sentence of two years, pending a successful completion of a drug rehabilitation program. The parole board decided that she could complete the final stretch at a Washington, D.C. halfway house, enabling her to return to her children. However, delays in paperwork within the Lexington FCI bureaucracy have interfered with her chance to go to the halfway house, embittering her toward the incompetent unit staff. "They constantly do people like this!" she says, and her face twists with frustration and pain. "They deliberately kept me here, after I spilled my guts out. I needed to be home with my children these past two months and they need me. I rather had even went as far as doing the rest of my time in the D.C. jail... at least they could come and visit...Lil Bit, she needs me."

Now, as her final date nears, Ne-Se plans out many details involved in regaining her independence and gathering her family together. "You gonna see, Kelly, just you wait and see. And you'll see me in Chicago, too, when Lil Bit and I come to visit you a year from now. And I'm gonna talk to those students you told me about. They'll listen to me. Yeah, I'll make 'em listen. And I'll show 'em these hands and these scars." She points to her legs. "Oh, Kelly, I can't wait to get out of this place. I can't wait."

EMANUELLE

The library is silent except for the squeaks of markers, as forty women sit quietly, coloring. "Do y'all have some smaller colors?" a plaintive voice calls out.

The PACT (Parents and Children Together) instructor comes to life. "No, these are the only colors we have." She shuffles through a stack of completed drawings, enclosed in plastic. "Now, here is a sample of a school bus colored in and made into a puzzle," she says, and begins to hand out black and white sketches of a school bus.

"We supposed to color these?" someone asks.

Ignoring the question, the PACT instructor continues in the exact tone she would use to address a roomful of five-year-olds coloring. "Here's one that has wheels, and here's one with hubcaps. Y'all pass it around now after ya' look at it."

"Hey, Ms, um, yeah, do you have any of them smaller colors?"

The question hangs unanswered. Now the PACT instructor wheels a videotape machine into the center aisle and switches on a video about the worth of getting a college education. Mothers at Lexington FCI go to PACT for one hour a month, mostly to color and watch videos. "We begin by building the basic blocks of an education," intones an authoritative commentator, whose voice and words have an effect similar to the white noise of Muzak.

Two tables away from me sits Emanuelle. She is one of several prisoners employed by the PACT program. Born and raised in France, a 29-year old mother of two, Emanuelle regularly imports fresh ideas for the PACT instructors; she draws from her own experience working in a Grenoble "house of animation," one of the numerous social centers French people provide for their children.

"Well," Emanuelle told me in Spanish choir practice one day, "I thought, yes, it would be a good idea to make tapes to send to our children, that this would not present too many problems, and the children would be so excited to hear from their mothers in that way, and, you know, for mothers who do not know how to write, this would be a help." On another occasion, she brainstormed about ways to help bring children to visit their mothers. I recall talking with her one day as she dusted empty tables in the PACT center. "Well," she said in a droll voice, "and what would happen if we were to sit around these tables?" She raised her impressive eyebrows and her pretty eyes danced. "Couldn't we talk with one another about our problems, about raising children, and learn from one another?!"

Most of her ideas are like seeds falling on dry ground. They are met with the same response as the petition for smaller markers. One proposal, however, appealed to the staff. Emanuelle volunteered to develop a coloring book, one that would depict mothers' circumstances in this prison. Since then, Emanuelle has been steadily sketching, rendering impressions of the courtyard, the cafeteria, the Big Yard. Her pictures will alleviate childrens' anxieties over imagined perceptions of prison. Emanuelle learned from experience that children need to know that their mothers eat decently, and that (unlike U.S. county jails), there is an absence of iron bars, and we do not idle the day away in dank, dark cells.

"The government wants educated citizens..." the tape plugging college educations drones on, as women color in the buses, "but it needs cooperation from an important source: YOU." I notice Emanuelle staring at me intently and wonder if a woman typing furiously, surrounded by several piles of folders and books, is about to become part of the coloring book.

Emanuelle has been especially lively and upbeat during the past four weeks, ever since her parents arrived from France. "Well, I have hope," Emanuelle says. "I don't want to be unrealistic, but I can see that some good things have happened, no?" She goes on to detail contacts made by her uncle, a French priest, which resulted in some attention being drawn to her situation. When she was first incarcerated in Puerto Rico, the uncle arranged for a bishop to visit her in the Puerto Rican jail. After a first contact, the bishop returned to celebrate a weekly liturgy with Emanuelle and others who wished to attend. After the shattering news of Emanuelle's four-year sentence arrived in France, her family and friends organized letter-writing campaigns on her behalf, and they began to plan trips to visit Lexington. Emanuelle's uncle, her brother, and now her parents, have received an outpouring of hospitality in this country. Local clergy found a spacious, comfortable house which the parents could occupy during their month's visit. Language and literature professors from the University of Kentucky planned receptions to welcome Emanuelle's parents. Contacts were made with legal counsel, which might be of some assistance. Emanuelle recognizes how sharply these gestures contrast with the aid available to the majority of the women here, most of whom are mothers who ache to see their children but cannot afford the costly visits.

I can't imagine that anyone here would begrudge Emanuelle her good fortune as regards outside support. Certainly she has been a support to countless women here. Reliant on gestures, smiles, and deeds to communicate with the English speaking population, Emanuelle has often motivated women to move beyond the confines of their rooms and the crushing boredom of passivity.

Her own days and nights are full, practicing with the Spanish choir, painting in the art gallery, studying English, fashioning beaded bracelets bearing peoples' names, maintaining a diary, and, with pen ever-ready, sketching. The deft, fluid strokes, as she rapidly outlines figures for her next watercolor, bespeak her graceful, energetic approach to living, even to life in prison. "Surely, I am not happy to be separated from my family," Emanuelle says, and her brow furrows momentarily. "But, I can find contentment here," she continues, matter-of-factly. "I have hope, yes. Still, if I must, I know I can do my four-year sentence and I will not stop living. In many ways, you know, I still have my freedom."

Emanuelle is intent upon using this time to become a better person. I think, to myself, that she will surely emerge a saint.

Her past includes a stretch of idyllic, carefree years, after she and her husband decided to follow "gypsy" travel urges and to adapt to the simple uncluttered lives of South American campesinos who live close to the land. They were interested in agriculture, cultural exchange, learning new languages, and cooperative ways to raise children. My Catholic, liberal friends speak often about a "preferential option for the poor," which we hope to exercise. Emanuelle's travels in Algerian, Turkish, Greek and Colombian villages have given her a very genuine understanding of that phrase. Her photos are fascinating, showing her and her husband to be extremely adaptable, and radiantly happy. I was especially impressed with photos from Turkey, wherein Emanuelle accepted segregation between men and women, deferring to the culture she had entered, and is pictured with her head modestly covered, posing with several other women on dilapidated wooden steps before a dark, simple Turkish dwelling.

Emanuelle comes from a family of conscientious objectors to war. Three of her brothers have refused military service. Her uncle works hard to further Middle East peacemaking efforts between villagers in Palestine and Israel. Her parents have opposed French interference in Algeria and Vietnam. Emanuelle believes it is wrong to pay for weapons, or to endorse others who might use murder and violence to achieve their own ends. We sort through current events in our leisurely strolls around the Big Yard, wondering often about means and ends as global conflicts hit the headlines. One day, Emanuelle spoke very sadly about a tragedy that occurred in France, in 1978. Non-violent disarmament groups had organized a huge "manifestation," calling for French withdrawal from the arms race. Some participants began throwing rocks. When a scuffle between police and demonstrators quickly escalated, one young man lost his life.

Emanuelle and her husband wanted to raise their two small children, now aged four and six, within a community that embraced values of simple living and harmony with nature. Their hopes were fulfilled when they discovered a mountain village in Colombia, where they lived for a year and a half, and then in Ecuador. They met with a severe crisis, however, when both children fell ill with fever and parasites. Frustrated and frightened by the chronic illness which the children seemed unable to shake, and wanting to begin their formal education, Emanuelle resolved to take the children to France for an extended visit. Their commitment to simple living left them strapped for cash. Proud of their independence, they were reluctant to ask their families for help funding Emanuelle's return trip. A friend proposed a remedy for their financial troubles. He suggested that Emanuelle carry a small amount of cocaine from Colombia to West Germany. The risk seemed minimal. At the time, Emanuelle was unaware of the toll cocaine usage had taken upon young people who easily became addicts. Now, she deeply regrets her naïveté. She cannot imagine ever repeating the same mistake.

The plane Emanuelle boarded was a direct flight between Colombia and West Germany. Unbeknownst to Emanuelle, however, United States Drug Enforcement Agents had planned an "emergency" touchdown in Puerto Rico, where agents would arrest anyone caught bearing drugs.

Awaiting trial in the Puerto Rican jail was a hellish time of anxiety, fear, and isolation for Emanuelle, until she was finally able to contact her family. She recalls constant shouting, outbreaks of violence, and miserable conditions. But Emanuelle says the most demoralizing experience, for her, occurred in the Miami airport, when she was being transported to the United States prison. She and other prisoners sat in the terminal, cuffed and chained together, entirely conspicuous. Passers-by, tourists, and vacationers stared at the bedraggled prisoners. "This was my first time in America," she said. " I cried the whole time, in that airport. They seemed so satisfied with their wealth, but I don't think they could recognize that wealth comes from having love and peace within. Some people are enslaved to money, clothes, swimming pools, these kinds of treasures. I am free because God gave me my freedom. Now, I identify with the apostles more, because I know we are different and we live apart in some ways."

By the time Emanuelle arrived here at Lexington FCI, she had already served eight months of the four-year sentence a Puerto Rican judge imposed on her after she pled guilty to a charge of possessing cocaine.

She speaks of how important the time for reflection has been. "I had reached a crossroads, a juncture, in my life, and, who knows, had I been successful in gaining that $7,000 profit as a drug transporter, perhaps I might have become a very different person. This experience has had an enormous effect on me and all my family."

Tears flow when Emanuelle speaks of her children. She longs to guide their growth, to be at her husband's side now while he struggles to work full-time and care for the children as a single parent. Biting her lower lip, she shows me the portrait she has completed of her and Matias, her youngest. The drawing shows them face-to-face, noses touching, stunningly beautiful profiles of love and tenderness. Soft curls and eager smiles give them both a pixie-like appearance.

Two weeks ago, Emanuelle approached me while I swept up debris in the Central Park courtyard. "Where will you be at 1:20 this afternoon?" she asked, eyes aglow. "Here," I replied. "Well, good, then you can sing a French song with me when the Concorde flies overhead. And I think it would be good if the plane dropped me a line and took me along." Emanuelle explained that the Concorde was a famous new plane that could travel from Paris to Lexington in three hours. She was going to ask for a pass to join me in the courtyard. As it turned out, Emanuelle couldn't get anyone to issue the pass. We decided that missing a chance to tip our hats to a plane made by a company so heavily invested in weapons production was no great loss anyway. The next day, I heard a roaring sound and looked up just in time to see the Concorde beginning its return trip to France. I imagined the passengers settling in for an enjoyable three-hour journey. No doubt their conversations would include mention of France's Bicentenary celebrations. Maybe they'd mention the French President's decision to offer a general amnesty to French prisoners, one that Emanuelle would have benefited from had she been charged in France. Actually, had Emanuelle appeared before French courts as a first time offender, she would not have been given more than six months probation. Instead, she has been punished U.S. style, condemned to four years of separation from her loved ones. The people on board the Concorde would reach France in less than three hours. For Emanuelle, the journey will take two-and-one-half more years.

ERNESTINA

Today Ernestina, a 62-year-old Mexican woman who has been one of my four roommates, reached the final day of her two-year sentence.

Yesterday, I accompanied her on her "merry-go-round," a series of required visits to the various prison departments. Prisoners must return any items issued by the institution and since Ernestina walks with a cane, I was allowed to carry her bags for her, some of which contained institutional clothing and some filled with bedding and shoes. We had thought she could take the institution's underwear with her. After all, what use would the prison have for it? At the R & D stop (Release and Delivery), where bags are checked, the guard snapped at Ernestina. "You can't take out that underwear. Go back to the laundry with it!"

"*Ay, chingada!*" Ernestina laughed softly as we left. I felt out of sorts over the stinginess we just witnessed, but Ernestina just invoked the words I've heard her use hundreds of times, which she says can't be translated into English, but come close to meaning "little fools." I was again struck by how lovable an "*abuelita*" (grandmother) Ernestina is.

For me, Ernestina's mere presence never fails to dispel the institution's colorless monotony. She looks like a female version Friar Tuck. Roly-poly, clad in simple dresses fashioned from sheets she has dyed pale blue and stitched with royal blue embroidery, she walks diffidently, always carrying a cane. Only a few gray strands are evident in her shiny, brown hair. Often, she ties her hair in a pony-tail using colorful knit covered rubber bands. (Women throughout the institution now use these hairbands, thanks to Ernestina's generosity and her ability to mass-produce hand knit items.)

Ernestina is jovial, loves to laugh and make others laugh. We've enjoyed teasing her.

She's the only person I've met who had a good word to say about the head of the Education Department, where she worked as an orderly. Ernestina even had a little crush on him, which sent the rest of us into whoops of laughter. He liked her cleverness. Plus, she was the most industrious worker in his department. I wonder if he knew about her Robin Hood-like tendencies to redirect departmental items. Each day, Ernestina would bring items from the storage room, redistributing them to people who needed envelopes, pens, folders, and paper, rarely, if ever, keeping anything for herself. I told her I expected to wake up one day with a copying machine beside my bed.

Ernestina's generosity is all pervasive. As I opened my mail, I would dutifully turn over any reusable portions of cards to her, so that she could give them to others. Yesterday, a post card arrived which depicted Gandhi holding a tiny triangle of salt in his cupped hand. "Do you want this one?" I asked.

Ernestina's brow furrowed and she crinkled her nose. "Why that man have cocaine?" she asked. I tried to explain the salt march to the sea, but soon she was laughing, and saying, "*Ay, chingada.*"

Lorenza, my Cuban roommate, and I had the morning off today, so we were able to have coffee and machine-bought rolls with our beloved Ernestina before she left. We were seated on our bunks, talking amiably, when the case manager and the counselor whisked into the room to stage an inspection. They searched for dust with the intensity of agents on a drug bust. They traced rims of mirrors, lockers, Venetian blinds, and the bulletin board. Ms. Montanez spoke into a hand-held tape recorder, "Room 104." Turning to Ms. Hedron, she shrugged and snorted, "Can't find any dust here." Ms. Hedron was running her hand between the lockers. "Well," she said disparagingly, glancing downward, "the floors aren't too terrific." Montanez spoke into the tape recorder, "Put down excellent. But add: floors need buffing."

They strutted off to look for dust in the next room. Ernestina's large, doe-like eyes followed them. I wondered if she felt hurt that they hadn't bothered to say good-bye or good luck. I wondered if the Case Manager had felt embarrassed over having refused to do the extra paperwork needed to secure a flight home for Ernestina. Did it cross her mind that this 62 year-old diabetic faced a 60-hour bus trip to California, with stopovers occurring only once every ten hours?

I dutifully pulled out the buffer, feeling resentful about polishing the floor during the few hours left with Ernestina. Lorenza cares about what the floors look like, and I try to do my part to keep the room in "excellent" condition. Lorenza spotted a patch of tile that still wasn't polished. "Lorenza," I said, *"la vida de una cucaracha tiene mas importancia, a mi, de sus pisos."* (I care more about the life of a cockroach than I do about their floors.) That tickled Ernestina, and she, giggling, repeated the line many times.

My remaining time spent with Ernestina helped me to piece together more of her life story. She knew I was on a "fishing expedition" yesterday when I asked her what her worst experience had been. "Why you ask?" she responded, a cloud of suspicion crossing her eyes. "Well," I said, "you seem so calm, always ready to make others feel better, and you rarely seem to feel down…"

"I pray every day, 'she said guardedly. "Every day I pray to God not to let me get sick here. When I'm outside here I always have lots of sickness. Here, no." Ernestina is an expert at diverting conversations.

"So, really," I said, "the hardest thing has been separation from your children, and the grandchildren." She nodded gravely. Ernestina raised several of the grandchildren since birth.

Today, she spoke more freely, perhaps because it was her last day, and she knew she needn't fear gossip. "When I first was in prison, everyday I stay in my room, shut the door, an' cry an' cry an' cry. I was so worried for my grandchildren. My daughter Gloria, that one, she kicked the young one, Cynthia, out of the house. Cynthia fourteen an' living on the street an' then she became pregnant. Well, she have miscarriage, but I was so worried. I thought there could be no God, or he wouldn't let this to happen."

Gloria is one of Ernestina's ten children. She and her brother, Lee, are both drug addicts. At age 21, Gloria discovered her husband shooting up. As Ernestina tells it, Gloria told the husband, "I want some. I want some. If you can use that, I can too." Speaking of Gloria, Ernestina says, "She has diabetes. When she was, how you say, hooked, she shoot the drugs right in front of me, and I thought it was insulin. For three years, you know. I never know. She steal from me and she trick me. Then one day, she tell me this guy tell her that if she take a truck full of marijuana from Mexico to here she get $7000. 'Yeah, Mama, I can use to buy us a washing machine and stereos,' she told me. And I told her, 'You are stupid! Don't do it!' But she keep up, so finally I said, O.K. Go! I'll take care of the kids.' She say 'It only gonna take 8 days.' And she took Cynthia, the daughter with her. Nine, ten, eleven days pass and I get a call from the American consul in Mexico. He say, 'Come and get your granddaughter,' He don't think it right that she should be in prison. They was in a Mexican prison. Gloria, she stay there for more than a year."

Lee, Ernestina's son, became hooked on drugs while serving with the U.S. military in Germany. He and his friends invited Ernestina to go with them, on vacation, from California to Mexico. They assured her they wouldn't take any detours to pick up marijuana.

"But why, " I asked, "why did they invite you?" I was perplexed.

"Because they thought no one would stop an old woman like me," Ernestina said, smiling slightly.

Wrong. Drug agents pulled the truck over. Lee now faces seven years and Ernestina was sentenced to two years in prison and eight years probation.

Gloria finished up her two-year sentence in the U.S., six months of which was spent here at Lexington, with Ernestina.

Ernestina worries now that she was a bad mother. She tells about her own childhood, when her mother tied a tight rope around her pants to prevent men from raping her. Once, she fought off a boss at the ranch where she worked, and she scarred his face badly. She was 11 years old then. Another time, while her mother was in the hospital giving birth, she had to resist her father. Not trusting the tight rope for protection, she grabbed her younger brother and headed for the family truck each night until her mother returned. She had left home shortly thereafter at age thirteen, seeking migrant farm work. She has been a manual laborer throughout her life.

Hoping to protect her children from the troubles she experienced, Ernestina set up strict rules about how late they could stay out, and how far from home they could go. "When they broke those rules, I beat them," she told me. She worked long hours at numerous jobs, eager to provide for all of their needs and many of their wants.

The child-raising years seem to have been full of frustrations, which multiplied as the children reached adulthood and began to bear their own children. Even when Gloria was 25 years old, Ernestina resorted to beating her up. "She come home, and she pale and look like she starve. It's because of the drug. So I give her $50 and I say, 'Now, go to the hospital.' When she come back, she tell me she spent the money on drugs. I grab her by the hair, and I throw her head this way and that. I beat her up. Then she went to the hospital."

A few weeks ago, a new arrival at Lexington carried news that Ernestina's husband of eight years had moved in with another woman, a white woman. I felt badly that my roommates chose to tease Ernestina about this. I knew that Ernestina's husband is a drug addict. She's clearly worried that he's using drugs again, and she guesses that the woman he moved in with supplied him with drugs. Ernestina speaks affectionately of him, observing that he's just like a little child, and very dependent on her. Her husband is blind, and she will be able to earn income by caring for him in the future. "He alone again," she confided in me two days ago. "And he's waiting for me because he know I'm the one to take care of him." I feel concerned and dubious, but I have no doubts of Ernestina's determined, loyal care for children and loved ones. At one point, when she was talking about parenting, I mentioned Thomas Gordon's book, *Parent Effectiveness Training*, and felt hopelessly bourgeois even as the words came out of my mouth. To my surprise, Ernestina and Lorenza both dove for a pen and paper to copy down the name of the book. They said they wanted to read anything that would help them better understand how to raise their children.

Noon came. I accompanied Ernestina on her final trip to R & D where the staff would search her bags once more, and then see her to the door. In their searching, would any of them recognize that they had encountered an "angel unawares?"

TERRY

When I first saw Terry, a statuesque woman who could easily pass for a model or a movie star, I registered a note of surprise because a staff person was treating prisoners so decently. Later, I learned that she was, herself, a prisoner.

Terry often helps people with legal concerns in the library. She frequently slips me clever or interesting items from the *Washington Post* or the *Miami Herald*. Her degree is in marine biology, but her range of interests seems inexhaustible. I marvel at the strength she brings to each new day. As I learned more of her story, I also began to marvel at her lack of bitterness.

"My thirty-year sentence was reduced to twenty years, " she recited, "so I've been down for five years and my release date is June of 1996." She was convicted of importing marijuana into the United States. Terry says she had been "retired" for four-and-one-half years; she'd remarried, and given birth to a child. She loved her new life, felt good about being completely detached from her "ex" and from the marijuana trade in which they'd been involved.

As with so many other cases, when the federal marshals came after her they had absolutely no regard for changes which she'd independently made since the days when she committed the alleged crime. Like many other women convicted of drug offenses, Terry was given a much longer sentence than any of the others involved in the trafficking. Her ex-husband, who had continued "working" and "brought in everything from Qualudes to cocaine" testified against her, as also did several of the other "kingpins."

"My ex got two years, but he refused to tell them where to find me after he testified against me. The feds went to his mother and told her that her son would get 70 years if she didn't tell them where to find me."

The mother asked, "Well, how much will Terry get?"

"Oh, she'll just get five years," the feds assured her.

Terry sighs as she tells it. "So, my mother-in-law was scared and turned me in. Her son got two years, and I got thirty."

Terry's new husband was killed in a plane crash. Her daughter, the child of the second marriage, was eighteen months old when Terry was arrested. "She's now six and a half," says Terry, "and in five years, I've seen her eight times. Pictures just don't compensate for her toddler years and her childhood." Terry lives in Antaeus, the dorm mainly occupied by pregnant women. "I can't imagine any worse torture than going through this place pregnant," Terry told me one day, after telling me about pregnant women sitting on the cold floors because all the furniture had been removed from the unit.

She's seen her share of prisons in the system. Initially, she spent three years in Pleasanton, California, even though her child lived in Virginia. Then, under the rent-a-cell program, she was shipped to the state of Washington. "It took the intervention of the sentencing judge and a senator to get me out of there. After ten months, I was transferred to Marianna, Florida, where they realized that my security level was too low to be in their maximum security prison and too high for camp placement, so I ended up here." Terry grimaced. "It's been a very rough five years...I've nothing to look forward to in the next five years, unless I get out of here."

We joke about finding the "Get Out of Jail Free" card in the library's law books. Terry constantly helps other women with their legal papers and seems to understand more than most. I watch her listen carefully to bewildered, devastated newcomers, and feel glad that someone has the energy to practice attentive listening skills and to be a counselor. Her patience and strength of spirit amaze me. Perhaps she learned her sense of self-discipline from her father, an Air Force colonel.

One day we talked about drug use. I felt tentative and hesitant about touching on the topic, anxious that if I told Terry about the sometimes fatal ramifications of drug traffic amongst the youngsters who were my neighbors and students in Chicago, she would feel I was judging her. My concerns were unnecessary. Terry listened to my anguish over Shawn and Cassius, two young friends and students of mine who were both killed shortly before the end of the previous school year. Presumably, they were shot by rival drug dealers. Terry shook her head thoughtfully. By now she's listened to a steady flow of drug offenders' stories. She articulates a compassionate, thoughtful analysis, drawing on connections between poverty and drug abuse. "Some people get into drugs because they don't have any other way to pay the rent, or to take care of their kids. What kind of job opportunities do people here have? The last "A & O" class (Admission and Orientation) took the basic skills test, and out of 58 people, only 14 placed higher than eighth grade."

"And what are kids supposed to think, when they know that people in the highest levels of government are involved in bringing drugs into the country?" Terry's maintained an avid interest in allegations about involvement of the CIA, and U.S. military operatives in smuggling cocaine and heroin into the United States in order to raise funds for U.S. sponsored paramilitary outfits, such as the contras. She distinguishes herself from those who traffic in heavy narcotics.

"We never got into that stuff. The stuff we sold just mellowed people out. How often do you read that a marijuana crazed driver caused a three car pile up or beat a spouse to a pulp?"

Chin on hand, Terry stares upward, through the library's open window, at clouds racing across a deep blue sky. "I could be doing a thousand things on the outside," Terry says dreamily. I easily believe her. "I raise Arabian horses," she murmurs. "I love the sea." Instead she sits here, behind the razor-wire fence, torn up over the situations of others and over her own unfair plight. And always the baffling question, "Why does a minor player get ten times the amount of time that the kingpins get, when she has only a fraction of the culpability?"

EARLINE

"Enough is enough is E-NOUGH!" Earline, a large black woman in her thirties, stares at the barbed wire fence just outside the window. She fingers a hastily-formed braid with one hand. She adjusts her glasses with the heel of her other hand.

"I'm sick and tired of this place. I want to go HOME to my KIDS." Earline intones these lines relentlessly, regularly, as though conjugating Latin verbs or reciting the state capitals of the U.S. In measured tones that speak volumes about her quiet and barely controlled desperation, she adds, "Don't these people know I'm supposed to be standing in a line with my kids, going to see Batman?"

When I first met Earline, we spent the evening talking about her children. Since then, she's divulged many stories about Stephen, eight, and Roland, who is three. Even amidst her worst spells of anxiety over being separated from her boys, Earline can't resist smiling and eventually laughing heartily when absorbed in a story about her children.

Stephen's latest craze revolves around rap music. Last night, Earline came to the library wielding a huge card depicting Mickey Mouse characters dancing "The Buck Wild," and delivering raps.

"Need any stamps?" I asked.

"No," Earline said. "I won't mail it out tonight...last night I mailed them the T-shirts I made for them, so I'll wait till Sunday to mail this." Earline constantly scavenges for creative items to send the boys. She would love to have daily phone contact with them, but their caretakers no longer accept her collect calls. Since her incarceration, ten months ago, the boys have been uprooted and moved to three different households. Often Earline feels frantic over notes from Stephen's teacher reporting uncontrollable behavior. A couple of months ago a friend let her know that Roland hasn't spoken to anyone for three weeks. Such reports fuel Earline's energy to spend almost every night in the library in a steady, industrious effort to find help for herself and her children. Earline has mailed out hundreds of letters appealing to congressional representatives, churches, prison support groups, legal aid groups, surrogate parent organizations, and most recently, the Oval Office. Sporadic responses arrive in the daily mail call. Most often, the letters evoke a resigned shrug from Earline. "Got the donut again," she tells me, handing a letter that typically begins, "We're sorry to inform you..." Still she persists.

Several months ago, Earline composed a generic "suffering letter." It narrates the tragic circumstances of a woman addicted to crack cocaine, but sentenced as a drug dealer by a court that refused to recognize her drug addiction. Earline was convicted on one count of conspiracy to distribute five grams of crack cocaine (about $500 worth of crack). The court imposed a mandatory five-year sentence without parole and four years of supervision. This was her first offense. Her pre-sentence investigation report indicates that she served in the United States Air Force for six active years (and two in reserve), attended college, and has been a stable homeowner in the Tampa area for several years. Earline's efforts to get herself out of prison seem, to me, to be motivated in part by a fundamental belief that the U.S. justice system couldn't possibly treat anyone so unjustly. In that sense, one might certainly say that she hasn't accepted being here.

"You haven't accepted the fact that you're in prison," the Case Manager chides Earline. "You're not adjusting." Actually, the Case Manager is riled because Earline's massive correspondence has generated additional paper work for the unit staff. The staff despises extra work; the Case Manager and Counselor are generally disgruntled about doing the bare minimum. Anytime an outsider inquires about an inmate, the Case Manager must fill out several forms in the process of responding. Earline has also submitted "cop-outs," formal requests for a transfer to the Mariana, Florida facility, where she could be closer to her children. The charge that Earline hasn't adjusted to prison life has led to a false conclusion that she is just plain maladjusted in general. The unit psychology intern, a university graduate student, filed a paper indicating that Earline is mentally unsuitable for a transfer to a camp. Had the young intern asked any inmate who knew Earline, she would have learned that Earline is regarded as one of the most mentally sound and stable people on the whole compound. The unit psychologist once confessed to me that she is very frightened, every day, when she must walk down the unit hallways to reach her office. "Face it," she said "I'm little and white." I tried to reassure her that no one was likely to jump her in the hallways. The student's inexperience in cross-cultural situations seems to me to have warped her perception of Earline, who is large and black. Without ever formally interviewing Earline or administering any tests, she was able to quash Earline's application process for a transfer. Earline's "cop-outs" in protest of the unfair evaluation have only netted renewed assurances from authorities that they regard her as being mentally unstable or as someone feigning mental instability.

Last weekend, I worried that the bureaucratic run-around and the Catch-22 imposed on Earline by the Psych department and the unit staff may finally be snuffing out her energies. "I'm jus' gonna' go to sick call and get me some drugs an' I'm gonna' go to bed, take drugs, an' I ain't gonna' write no more letters, jus' go to sleep an' one day they'll wake me up an' say 'Go Home'."

Such malaise contrasts starkly with the attitude Earline had when we first met. Six months ago, she was energetically compiling a collection of "100 Facts About Black History;" she would devour library materials about art history (another passion of hers). Back then, Earline was alert to the events of the day, both within and beyond the compound.

A restful weekend plus kindly but firm assistance from several close friends helped Earline retrieve her will power and muster perseverance to face another week away from home.

"Home" has warm, positive connotations for Earline. She fondly remembers her own parents who "did the best they could with what they had." George Washington, her father, instilled fierce pride in his children during their childhood years in Providence, Rhode Island. Earline recalls the standards he expected Margaret, their mother, to maintain. George Washington's children must be neatly dressed, and NOT in second hand clothes. "'Where did you get that dress from, girl, ' he'd ask," Earline says with imitation gruffness. "If you said "the Goodwill," that dress had to go IN the TRASH!"

"He was a gambling man and he was real lucky at the race track," Earline continues. He was also a steady, hard worker, employed in construction business and, later, running a popular club in Providence," the place for black people to dress up and go someplace nice...there was no fighting and no getting loud."

"My father was a generous, warm-hearted man." Earline's eyes glow as she reminisces about her father throwing an annual picnic for the whole neighborhood, hosting yearly brunches on Mothers' Day, and sponsoring the local Little League team.

Earline's mother, a nurse, was emphatic about education. "Going out dancing and stuff was good, but she had rather seen you with a BOOK." George always insisted that Margaret take the children to local events, and so Earline regularly went to the circus, the Ice Capades, the Harlem Globetrotters, and premiers of new movies. "And we always took a little vacation to some place every year."

Earline inherited George and Margaret's values about child-rearing. Wanting to imbue Stephen with pride in his heritage, she spent a summer traveling with him to places that he would one day read about in black history studies. They traced the Underground

Railroad routes as part of the trip. When the children came to visit Earline in prison, they easily slipped into a dance routine that the three of them learned to do at home. "You're the background, Noel!" Kristopher repeated in a stage whisper, gently trying to nudge little Noel to the back, as Earline and Stephen glided through the routine.

Earlier, Earline encouraged Stephen to think about places he'd like to go to when she returns. "Naw." he said, "I don't wanna go any-where. I just want to stay home and dance like we used to."

Watching Earline and her children together was a treat, especially within the sterile confines of a prison visiting room. Roland's chubby arms encircled his mother's neck lovingly as he clambered into her lap. Stephen placed an arm around her broad shoulders and leaned his head on hers.

Earline is transparently filled with desire and energy to continue caring for her children. Herein, the harvest of those very energies, however, inevitably becomes deepened by anguish over separation, plus a sense of futility over her inability to control circumstances affecting herself and her children.

Perhaps it was Earline's grandmother who best summed up a fun-damental irony of Earline's situation here. Puzzled over Earline's long sentence, she expressed her frustration when Earline called to wish her a happy birthday. "Child, I just don't understand! You got five years and ain't nobody dead yet!

Outsiders who visit the prison as guest lecturers seem particularly insensitive to that anguish and futility. Earline never misses the ironies that lace their talks. After Rosy Grier, the football star addressed women here, Earline returned to the unit with her familiar quizzical expression and mused aloud. "Why is it that every time a preacher comes here, he tells us that we're free? I have to write to Michael Quinlan (head of the Bureau of Prisons) about that. If I'm free, as they always say I am, then what's the problem? Why can't I walk out the door?"

On another occasion, the Governor of Kentucky's wife, Martha Wilkinson, spoke at a graduation ceremony that Earline and I attend-ed. "We're all in this together," Mrs. Wilkinson assured us, at the beginning of her talk. "I'm going to talk about where you've been and where you're going," she continued.

"Hmmph!" Earline grunted. "She don't wanna mention where we're at!"

"No one is in control of your life but you," the Governor's wife stated, going on to guarantee us that the entire staff is here for our positive reinforcement, that the sky's the limit for positive thinkers, and that we must always be willing to tell the truth. Ms. Wilkinson then slipped into her standard drug rap. "Drugs and alcohol are the most powerful forces in our lives," she claimed.

Earline poked me. "They ain't what's gonna end human history. It's those bombs you're always talking about, Ms. Kelly!"

Ms. Wilkinson's voice became even more sugary. "I'm interested in hearing from ALL of you." Earline scribbled a note on her program.

"Send suffering letter," it read.

Every prisoner I've known dreamed of release and reunion with loved ones. Many women at Pekin FCI thought hard about how their dreams could be realized if there were substantial reforms in the criminal justice system. Below are reflections distilled from steady discussions with several prisoners. We agreed these ideas should be written in hopes that readers would entertain what for the women I left behind is a searing question: Are there alternatives?

Are there alternatives?
June 2004

I wrote these reflections about alternatives to prison from inside a prison library, mostly on quiet Sunday mornings, following long and thoughtful discussions with women who care deeply about the issue. Several had maintained careful research files on prison reform, sentencing reform, and prison abolition. Each of the women I spoke with on the issue could easily have fit into any work place or community I know of in "mainstream America." I've met women who could have been my next-door neighbors, co-workers, sisters-in-law and work supervisors on the outside. This is my effort to bring people on the outside their voices.

To begin with, 82 per cent of the women at Pekin are first-time offenders convicted of nonviolent crimes. Over half of the women here are long-termers facing eight or more years of imprisonment. At the medium-high-security prison for men next door to us, the average sentence is twenty-five years. Back in 1989, when I was in maximum-security prison, sentences of over eight years seemed rare to us. Mainstream America seldom notices that the prison population has quadrupled over the past twenty years. Two million one hundred thousand people are locked up in federal and state prisons here in the land of the free, more than in any country in the world, or in world history. Over half of the world's prisoners are in U.S. prisons. Are there alternatives?

Not without a serious change in the American mindset. Myths about all criminals as dangerous sociopaths who belong behind bars have fostered a "throw away the key" mentality in the U.S. Most people in the U.S. believe current structures are legitimate and can't be dismantled.

In addition, a strong network of well-paid professionals derives profit and prestige from the status quo of "the prison-industrial complex." Judges, lawyers, prison architects, wardens, owners, and executives of companies with lucrative prison contracts—all have an investment in maintaining their roles. Those who teach and practice law enforcement at many levels have acquiesced to the current system and seem disinclined to recommend necessary changes.

Finally, lawmakers themselves have found that promises to be "tough on crime and crack down on drugs" help them win elections.

Before asking whether we should change the prison system, perhaps we must ask: is there even a hope that we could build a movement to do it? No one has publicly processed the social pain caused by locking up 2.1 million people. And yet each prisoner has relatives and friends who would welcome the idea that the U.S. prison system was not an absolute necessity. If organized, such groups could become a significant voting bloc. Joined by practitioners of nonviolence who refuse to accept the current arrangements, they could collectively ask a question nearly always posed by reformers and revolutionists: are the current arrangements absolutely necessary or are they contrived?

Admittedly, any groups campaigning to change this system face a monumental challenge. I will argue, as will many of my former fellow prisoners alongside me, that what is needed is the abolition of much of our prison system.

"Abolition" is very much the word here. The odds against abolition of prisons resemble the odds against early abolitionists determined to dismantle slavery or the odds faced by sharecroppers, students and a handful of ministers determined to abolish segregation and Jim Crow laws in the U.S. But these campaigns were successful, and the campaign for radical prison reform—prison abolition—could also be successful. How would it work?

A necessary first step would be to redirect current military expenditures into funding to meet human needs, liberating approximately 400 billion dollars each year. Along with that vast sum of money, we could also anticipate freeing up the richness of talents, research capacities, innovative thinking and enmeshing of various disciplines which is now commandeered by the U.S. military.

Drawing from those resources, "problem solvers" would be given incentives to develop the necessary structures for confronting crime and fostering restitution and community safety, and for rehabilitating individuals and groups guilty of endangering the common good.

Let's clarify what that common good entails. What actions pose the greatest threats to U.S. people and to the survival of our planet?

Topping any rational list would be the development, storage, sale, and threatened use of nuclear weapons, along with the stockpiling and use of chemical, biological and conventional weapons. Our weapons, in our hands and others, have caused massive death, destruction, maiming, orphaning, and poisoning in every part of the globe. Unbridled U.S. military expenditures have engendered global arms races which have further cost millions of lives through trillions of misspent dollars and lost resources which could have been used to eradicate poverty, hunger, and disease. The producers and potential users of these weapons walk the streets, free to continue their terrifying weapon buildup, while Lupe and Emanuelle remain behind bars.

Again, a sea-change in the public's mindset is necessary here, and achievable.

Ask environmentalists to specify actions that threaten the survival of our planet and they will likely discuss the devastation caused by producing acid rain and other pollutants, depleting the topsoil, overconsuming irreplaceable resources, and failing to maintain ecosystems necessary for survival on our planet.

Social scientists would point to the statistics showing drunk driving as a major cause of death in the U.S. health care professionals could point to sale of addictive and lethal products like cigarettes. The National Center of Addiction and Substance Abuse collects data on cost to states of tobacco, alcohol, and other drug addictions. Tobacco and alcohol addictions create the greatest costs. And who is working to addict people to cigarettes and alcohol? Are they likely to end up behind bars?

Collectively, these unpunished offenders cause more death and destruction than the worst incarcerated criminals. Putting polluters and weapons manufacturers in prison won't stop the problem. Efforts to stop the real threats to our survival and health would require greater ingenuity and determination.

The question should be, how do we deal with lethal behavior as a whole?

"Truth and reconciliation committees" of the sort formed after the demise of dictatorships, are necessary for healing our society in which so many have been powerless by crime in high places. These would help communities heal from damage inflicted on them by the profiteers of lethal behavior. And they would be a model for societal healing from other crimes, as well.

One of the worst industrial accidents in history, and one of the most atrocious unpunished crimes, occurred in Bhopal, India when a Union Carbide plant released a highly toxic cloud of poison gas, methyl isocyanate, into the atmosphere. (States like Illinois and Texas are full of plants storing gases that might cause the next Bhopal-style disaster). Fair reparations have never been made, and the survivors have never received adequate health care.

How would a just society—or a society that wanted to be safe from further disasters—handle this crime? First, a truth and reconciliation committee would make the truth known publicly and generate political pressure for restitution. Dow Chemical, the company that now owns the Union Carbide plant, would be made to enter into fair negotiations with the communities still affected by the plant disaster. Oversight committees would assure that the communities were compensated and that the surrounding land and water were decontaminated.

If we won't take care of these basic corrective procedures, how can we talk about jail for the people I met in prison?

When we seek out individuals to punish, such scapegoating creates a smokescreen that obscures wider social responsibility for ongoing crime. Tracking down and punishing the individual Union Carbide executives would only help to hide the responsibilities we in the First World collectively incur by living comfortably while exploiting the resources of places like Bhopal, India.

Suppose we agreed not to imprison weapons manufacturers for mass or serial murder. We could follow the truth and reconciliation model—we would make them enter negotiations to direct their resources toward socially useful projects. Scientists, engineers, and researchers would assist in rehabilitating the weapon making companies to design valuable end products such as mass transit or irrigation systems. Similarly, officers of tobacco manufacturing companies wouldn't be imprisoned for selling death-dealing products and even marketing them to children. Rather, they would be assisted to direct their resources toward health care and detoxification centers.

A reader might object that this discussion doesn't pertain to the population actually inhabiting U.S. prisons. Again, it's important to ask who or what actually poses major threats to us, to our children, and to the future of the planet. It's not likely to be the "criminal" who, possibly out of desperation to get an economic stake in an impoverished community, participated in the underground economy of that community and sold drugs to someone else in the community.

Who does go to prison? One million two hundred forty thousand prisoners—well over half of the 2.1 million people imprisoned in the U.S. federal and state prison systems—are charged with nonviolent crimes. Seventy-eight per cent of these prisoners have committed drug-related crimes. According to Families Against Mandatory Minimums (FAMM), half the federal and state prisoners serving mandatory minimum sentences are first time-offenders.

Many of these prisoners are themselves addicts. Rehabilitation is far more cost-effective than incarceration, yet woefully under-funded. Some manner of rehabilitation would be necessary for all criminals, from the weapons manufacturer down to the small-time financial crook.

Again, the model would be truth and reconciliation. Wise and compassionate educators and students would work, constantly, to rationally and systematically assess behaviors that jeopardize the human community. Their evaluations would be democratically managed and open to the air of public opinion and community scrutiny.

In some extreme cases of people who have treated other people abusively, we may need to contemplate removing the abuser from his or her intended victim. Suppose someone suffers from the disease of pedophilia. He or she should not be allowed to live or work with children, which would mean a level of removal from mainstream society. But it should not mean placement in a setting that dehumanizes, takes away almost every choice-making function, punishes any act of dissent or independence, and makes life so bland and uninteresting that the offender must struggle, every day, against an overwhelming desire to escape.

Why not imagine well-structured but non-abusive alternative communities where workers would live and work as guides and counselors? The employees would be well-educated, well-remunerated, and held to high professional standards. They would agree never to carry armaments and would understand, before signing up, that their choice to join the community would entail the same risks as countless other dangerous and well-remunerated jobs. These communities would be small, never risking becoming places that require bureaucracies to "process" the residents. The economic, social and cultural patterns within these places would be characterized by egalitarianism as much as possible. Authority would be earned by those who demonstrate the best leadership skills. When inhabitants of the communities had grievances, these would be aired and communicated well outside the community so that exposure to the wider world would enable discovery of ways to heal the grievance.

In the relatively short span of time, since WW II, the Catholic Worker movement has grown to include well over one hundred houses of hospitality in the U.S. and other countries. These houses are dedicated to caring for the neediest people in our societies without imposing on them a set of expectations beyond several basic demands. Guests are treated with acceptance, and generally the people maintaining the house don't try to "fix" the guests. However, they are not allowed to come into the house intoxicated and they can't store, use, or sell drugs or alcohol inside the house.

What strikes me as especially hopeful in this movement is the constant flow of young volunteers who are drawn to move into the communities, knowing they will not be paid a salary or, in most cases, even a modest stipend. Many of the young volunteers work part-time jobs to help cover household expenses.

Each house has its own set of rules and routines. You won't find a hierarchy in the Catholic Worker movement. You will find tremendous dedication to "the further invention of nonviolence", small and energetic groups of people who are learning to live simply and sensibly. They are some of the most joyful and enjoyable people you could ever hope to encounter.

I include this digression to indicate that it would be possible to find idealistic young people to work willingly in alternative communities.

We would need teachers and students to help accomplish a tremendous shift in values, here in the U.S. and in other Western countries, and we must recognize the importance of awakening a new social imagination that will mobilize young people to feel comfortable doing work they find meaningful, even if it doesn't allow them to accumulate excess personal wealth.

Other Lands Have Dreams

Suppose that our future promising students could find rewards in being highly trained specialists who could design humane communities for rehabilitation, recovery, ongoing assistance to "ex-offenders," and, in extreme cases, maintenance of the alternative communities mentioned above. Students who have enjoyed advantages in their upbringing would be prepared to answer a difficult question: Why would people who already have so much be entitled to get more?

Accomplishing any of these ideals would require a new generation of teachers and students motivated by new social imaginings and a belief that reforms are possible. I find it ironic that some of the most promising dialogue I have heard regarding crucial social issues came from within the confines of an isolated prison. Women clinging to the dream of finally hearing "two days an' a wake-up" signaling their release from prison deliberate over ideas that could point us all toward that sweet land of liberty we'd like to think we inhabit.

PART FOUR

Horizons and Hopes

N NOVEMBER 2003, CLOSE TO 14,000 PEACEFUL PROTESTERS ASSEM-
bled at the gates of Fort Benning, Georgia to demand closure of
the Western Hemisphere Institute for Security (WHINSEC), formerly named School of the Americas (SOA), a military combat training school located on the base. I was among twenty-seven activists
who stepped onto a few feet of the base, carrying crosses to com-
memorate people murdered by WHINSEC/SOA graduates.

We were arrested, handcuffed, and bused to what looked like an
empty warehouse where we would be "processed." Anticipating a procedure not very different from airport security searches, I noncha-
lantly awaited my turn to enter the large room. I was directed to
Station J where several Military Police stood, one of whom held a clip-
board and seemed to be supervising. Below is an article I wrote about
how U.S. Army Military Police responded when I quietly refused to
cooperate with an extremely aggressive search procedure. I was
pushed to the floor, hogtied, kneed while begging for relief because I
couldn't breathe, hauled hogtied to the next "stations," and threatened with pepper spray if I didn't cooperate when uncuffed for fin-
gerprinting.

It's important to note in the following article that one of the soldiers treated me kindly. It's also important for me to remember that
those of my former students who "hung out" on the streets of
Uptown, in Chicago, and were often picked up by the police would be
all too familiar with this story. I think they'd ask, "So what else is
new?!"

Nevertheless, the story prompts serious questions about the kind
of training we invest in as we increasingly rely on military strength
when dealing with foreign lands.

Public Relations spokespeople for the WHINSEC claim that the
school has been reformed and now teaches Latin American soldiers
the same standards of respect for human rights and civil law practiced
by the U.S. military. How can they possibly teach respect for human

rights or set a good example for Latin American soldiers when, for purposes of intimidation, they themselves respond to nonviolent protest with physical abuse? If this is what the U.S. Army MPs will do, with witnesses present, to a graying 105 pound peace activist in full view of priests and nuns as witnesses, in the context of an annual protest which has always been entirely peaceful, imagine what the trainees would do in a far away place, like Iraq, where they are under extreme pressures but can also act without witnesses.

Hogtied and Abused at Fort Benning
December 2, 2003

On Sunday, November 23, I took part in a nonviolent civil disobedience action at Fort Benning to protest the U.S. Army's School of the Americas (SOA, now remarketed as the Western Hemisphere Institute for Security Cooperation, WHINSEC).

Shortly after more than two dozen of us entered Fort Benning and were arrested, U.S. Military Police took us to a warehouse on the base for "processing." I was directed to a station for an initial search, where a woman soldier began shouting at me to look straight ahead and spread my legs. I turned to ask her why she was shouting at me and was ordered to keep my mouth shut, look straight ahead, and spread my legs wider. She then began an aggressive body search. When ordered to raise one leg a second time, I temporarily lost my balance while still being roughly searched and, in my view, "womanhandled." I decided that I wouldn't go along with this dehumanizing action any longer.

When I lowered my arms and said, "I'm sorry, but I can't any longer cooperate with this," I was instantly pushed to the floor. Five soldiers squatted around me, one of them referring to me with an expletive (this f—-er) and began to cuff my wrists and ankles and then bind my wrists and ankles together. Then one soldier leaned on me, with his or her knee in my back. Unable to get a full breath, I gasped and moaned, "I can't breathe." I repeated this many times and then began begging for help. When I said, "Please, I've had four lung collapses before," the pressure on my back eased. Four soldiers then carried me, hogtied, to the next processing station for interrogation and propped me in a kneeling position. The soldier standing to my left, who had been assigned to "escort" me, told me that soon the ankle and wrist cuffs, which were very tight, would be cut off. He let me know that he would have to move my hair, which was hanging in front of my face, so that my picture could be taken. I told him I'd appreciate that.

Moments later, he gently squeezed my shoulder. I won't forget that.

I was then carried to the next station. There, one of the soldiers who'd pushed me to the floor knelt in front of me and, with his nose about two inches from mine, told me that because I was combative I should know that if I didn't do exactly as instructed when they uncuffed one hand, he would pepper spray me. I asked him to describe how I'd been combative, but he didn't answer.

After the processing, I was unbound, shackled with wrist and ankle chains, and led to the section where other peaceful activists, also shackled, awaited transport to the Muskogee County jail. At our bond hearing the next day a military prosecutor told the federal judge that the military was considering an additional charge against me for resisting arrest. I explained my side of the story to the judge, grateful that there were at least several witnesses upon whom I could call.

The federal judge determined that most of us were "flight risks" and increased by 100 per cent the cash bond required before we could be released, from last year's $500 to $1000.

Today I have a black eye and the soreness that comes with severe muscle strain. Mostly, I'm burdened with a serious question, "What are these soldiers training for?" The soldiers conducting that search must have been ordered not to tolerate the slightest dissent. They were practicing intimidation tactics far beyond what would be needed to control an avowedly nonviolent group of protesters who had never, in thirteen years of previous actions, caused any disruption during the process of arrest. Bewildered, most of us in the "tank" inside the Muskogee County jail acknowledged that during the rough processing we wondered, "What country do we live in?" We now live in a country where Homeland Security funds pay for exercises which train military and police units to control and intimidate crowds, detainees, and arrestees using threat and force.

This morning's aches and pains, along with the memory of being hogtied, gave me a glimpse into the abuses we protest by coming to Fort Benning. As we explore the further invention of nonviolence in our increasingly volatile time, it's important to resolutely oppose training military people to use reactionary methods designed to humiliate, intimidate and punish civilians.

GENERATION KILL?

In January 2004, Judge G. Mallon Faircloth sentenced me to three months in prison for the November 2003 protest. During three days of trial, my twenty-six co-defendants offered moving testimony about why they carried crosses and coffins onto the base. They spoke on behalf of people whose voices can never be heard in U.S. courts, the voices of those who've been wounded, orphaned, maimed, disappeared, and murdered because of U.S. militarism.

We heard stories of military atrocities, carried out by graduates of a U.S. military combat training school, that helped explain why increasing numbers of people in other parts of the world feel seething rage and antagonism toward the U.S.

Speaking in August, 1990 as the U.S. began mobilizing for the 1991 Operation Desert Shield war against Iraq, the first President Bush, said: "Our jobs, our way of life, our own freedom and the freedom of friendly countries around the world would all suffer if control of the world's great oil reserves fell into the hands of Saddam Hussein."

Following that war, at a 1992 energy conference in Rio de Janeiro, the first President Bush told the representatives assembled that "the American way of life is non-negotiable."

Twelve years later, led by the second President Bush into unending war and increasing poverty, an unwillingness to change a dangerously wasteful lifestyle has locked U.S. people into a terrible conundrum.

Enormous talent, creativity, and money are poured into military spending, ostensibly to defend us. Is the lifestyle enjoyed by the majority of people in the U.S. defensible? From the perspective of people lacking access to basic necessities, the American way of life seems impossible to defend.

People living in lands rich in resources which the U.S. wants to control and exploit may find that unless they are willing to subordinate themselves to U.S. national interests, the U.S. will use its superior military might to punish them into submission. Our non-negotiable lifestyle translates into thousands dead.

Meanwhile, Western culture continues an ongoing war against Mother Earth as we contaminate the water, land, and air, ravage the soil, and burn fossil fuels.

A reporter embedded with Marines in Operation Shock and Awe described many of the Marines he met in the platoon as "socially maladjusted, heavily armed, and an international liability." This doesn't cohere with my own experience of Marines who occupied the intersection outside the Al Fanar hotel, after they spearheaded the blitz from the Kuwait border into Baghdad. Many of those Marines told us they regretted the suffering they'd seen, asked us to tell them our side of the story, and said they wished they could be part of rebuilding Iraq. I think the embedded reports of both the journalists and the peace activists are honest accounts, but referring to military people sent to Iraq as "Generation Kill," (the title of one embedded reporter's memoir of Operation Shock and Awe) gives me pause. Better to include multiple U.S. generations in that appellation.

If we've adjusted to possessing an arsenal of weapons that could destroy the planet, if we've adjusted to a lifestyle that pillages the Earth's resources while we spend trillions of dollars on weapons that aren't necessary to defend the continental United States, if we've acquiesced to a foreign policy based on the doctrine of "preventive war," then we are ourselves a heavily armed, maladjusted, international liability.

Elected officials often perceive that we put them in power to protect our inordinately comfortable lifestyles, and if they have to use violent means to do so, we will foot the bill. Refusal to pay for war (through war tax resistance) and readiness to radically resist militarism through nonviolent means helps us find what Rev. Miguel D'Escoto pointed us toward: "nonviolent actions commensurate to the crimes being committed."

Suppose we were to redirect just one billion dollars from our military budget to train doctors, nurses and water specialists who would be sent abroad, with no strings attached, to assist in neighboring countries? Wouldn't our security be enhanced if people in other lands viewed us as compassionate and generous people no longer addicted to war?

Getting Together to Defeat Terrorism
Step 1: Look in the Mirror
March 19, 2004

Following the March 11, 2004, terrorist attacks in Madrid, Secretary of State Colin Powell told ABC TV's "This Week" that he hoped Europeans, recognizing that no one is immune, would dedicate themselves to "going after" terrorist organizations with military force, intelligence, and law enforcement. He said that all of us have to get together to defeat organizations determined to kill and destroy innocent people. He urged Spain to stay in Iraq, and not to retreat from "the war on terrorism."

I think a crucial step forward in coming to grips with terrorism requires that we ask ourselves why individuals, some of them young, rational people with their whole lives ahead of them, would hate the U.S. and its allies so much that they would commit acts of massive destruction and end their own lives as well.

Shortly after U.S. troops began occupying Iraq in April, 2003, a large contingent of western media people arrived in Baghdad. One young journalist said a more seasoned correspondent had told her to talk with me when she was ready to do a humanitarian story. One of the first stories she pursued was about a baby who'd been born in one of Saddam Hussein's prisons. I suggested she might also explore stories about the hundreds of thousands of children who died because of economic sanctions. "Oh," she said, "that was Saddam Hussein's fault." I mentioned that U.N. documents showed that economic sanctions contributed to the deaths of over 500,000 children under age five. Her response was immediate: "Well, except now everyone knows that the U.N. was in bed with Saddam Hussein."

U.S. think tanks helped brief U.S. journalists before they headed over to the war zone. Perhaps the complex U.S./U.N. relations during thirteen years of economic sanctions couldn't have fit into convenient briefings. With deadlines to meet, electrical outages to cope with, and editors seeking stories about Saddam's cruelties, who could expect this young, energetic reporter to delve into analysis of yesteryear's news?

But if U.S. people are ever going to understand what would motivate people to end their lives committing gruesomely destructive acts, we'll have to step back from what the mainstream media dishes out to us, and strive for empathy, try to understand why terrorists believe it's imperative to resist U.S. domination. One way to develop such empathy would be to revisit the history of Iraq under economic sanctions and military bombardment.

If the U.S. had wanted to help Iraqis eventually defy the regime and move toward more democratic governing structures, it would have worked to strengthen Iraq's education systems, bolster capacity for communication, and develop social services. Instead, thirteen years of economic sanctions wrecked Iraq's education, cut people off from communication beyond and often even within Iraq, and drastically reduced social services, making people continually more dependent on the regime for subsistence.

After five years of Oil-for-Food, it was clear that the U.S. was simply interested in finding excuses to maintain sanctions. Despite incredibly detailed levels of monitoring and documentation by U.N. officials across every agency working in Iraq, the U.S. continued to pretend that the Iraqi government could solve a massive health care crisis by distributing hoarded medicines. Despite repeated U.N. agency claims that Iraqis didn't have adequate medicines and medical relief supplies, the U.S. continued to maintain that Saddam Hussein's regime was solely responsible for suffering because it refused to use the money and medicine it had available.

The truth is that no amount of medicine could have saved the lives of children then, and that it still won't be adequately effective, because Iraq's infrastructure is so badly debilitated that even now, infant mortality at the neonatal clinic in the Yarmuk Hospital in Baghdad is twice that of last year. And at Baghdad's Central Teaching Hospital for Children, where gallons of raw sewage wash across the floors, the hospital's doctors say, "The hospital drinking water is contaminated," and, "80 per cent of patients leave with infections they did not have when they arrived." (Jeffrey Gettleman, "Chaos and War Leave Iraq's Hospitals in Ruins," *New York Times*, February 14, 2004.)

Many of the accounts about ways that Saddam Hussein's regime engaged in smuggling and arranged kickbacks under the Oil-for-Food program were widely reported while Saddam Hussein's regime was still in power. We should be scandalized by that regime's choice to live luxuriously when they could have helped save the lives of innocent children. And we should be equally scandalized that the U.S. used the U.N. to wage economic warfare against Iraq, knowing full well that the sanctions would target and punish innocent people, including children, who had no control over their government.

In Baghdad, a few days before the Shock and Awe war began, a woman whom I've known for seven years whispered, "Believe me, Kathy, we want this war. All the people, they are tired of this life where we work so hard and still cannot feed our children." A March 9, 2004 letter from her explains how betrayed and battered she now feels. "Today, we faced a horrible day. My partner, the engineer, was attacked by shooting. He was wounded by three shots and is in the hospital. We are not sure if he will live. This is Iraq today. This is what we pay for Mr. Bush and his freedom. We can't move from place to place without shooting and bombing. We are like hostages in our own land. There is no safety, no jobs, no good water, no electricity. Everything is bad here. We are hopeless. We can't protect our children."

Other Lands Have Dreams

I wonder if people who flocked to see Mel Gibson's *The Passion of the Christ* understand that the brutality Jesus suffered was the same as punishment, under Roman occupation, for those convicted of insurrection. Military occupation then and now is not much different. Imagine anyone in Iraq, Israel, or Palestine, whether civilian or military, occupier or occupied, who survives a bombing, their limbs shattered, organs ripped open, flesh torn. Imagine arms aching for loved ones who'll never return. Or imagine someone armless and yearning, like the woman whom Faith Fippinger wrote of who had given birth to a baby just before a U.S. bomb tore off her arms during the Shock and Awe campaign. Other women helped the armless woman nurse the infant by crouching behind her and holding the baby to her breast.

I recently read about a woman who carried her sister-in-law's newborn baby to a hospital where she had been advised that an incubator would be available. When she arrived, she learned another woman had arrived before her and the incubator was taken. A nurse tried to console the distraught woman, but her companion, the mother's sister, was willing to try an alternative. Using a manual ventilator, she followed a nurse's instructions: "Squeeze and let go, squeeze and let go, as long as she could. Shortly before dawn, after standing by the baby and working the respirator for eight hours, Mehdi's arms gave out." (*Washington Post*, "Iraqi Hospitals on Life Support," March 5, 2004.) The baby died of respiratory failure.

I don't know anyone in Iraq who wasn't relieved to see Saddam Hussein deposed. I'd like to be heartened by those who say they advocated warfare against Iraq because they wanted to save Iraqis from an abusive despot. But I can't help but wish that this profound care for Iraqi people could have been activated during the long years when Iraqis endured sanctions.

Why do some people in the Islamic world hate us so much? It's a quick discussion. We take over and dominate other people's societies. We set up client states in their regions and rely on these client states to house U.S. bases. We foster double standards, condemning invasion and occupation when it suits us (e.g., the Iraqi invasion of Kuwait) and yet undertaking or supporting murderous sanctions, invasions, and occupations, while claiming to support and enhance democratic states. Hideous and violent terrorist attacks will continue as long as we insist on taking other people's precious and irreplaceable resources for cut-rate prices. We should either begin paying fair prices, or find new ways to live in which we're not so dependent on these resources.

How could we live differently, with less consumption and waste? Let me answer for myself. I consume far more than my fair share of jet fuel, electrical energy, and water each year. It's time to start rationing myself. The old adage, "Live simply so that others can simply live" comes to mind.

I'll have a refresher course in simple living during the late spring and summer of this year when I'll be an inmate in a U.S. federal prison for four months. The prison-industrial complex is a cruel extension of U.S. war-making against the poor in our country, but I hope this prison sentence, for nonviolent trespass on U.S. military installations, will serve me as an incubation period, a time of adjustment while living with less, and a time to hatch new ideas about how to live more simply after I leave the prison.

I hope all of us will find ways to slow down, find more leisure time, and in our times of rest reflect very seriously on Colin Powell's encouragement that we "get together to defeat organizations determined to kill and destroy innocent people." I hope we can get together to nonviolently defeat U.S. militarism, at home and abroad.

Step 2: Think of the Children
November 29, 2004

In the past year, several groups have asked me to facilitate retreats for people who want to further explore nonviolence. At the retreats, I ask volunteers to role-play situations likely to generate discussion about challenges people face when involved in peace activism. One of the most reliably difficult scenarios stages a spouse raising with his or her partner a decision to become a war tax refuser and stop paying federal income tax.

In one such scene, an anguished husband implored his wife to understand his reasons for stopping payment of federal income tax. "How could you do this to our children?" she asked. "And why didn't you think of this before you became a father?" The husband responded, "Honey, I just want to do something for peace," to which the wife blurted out, "At Christmas?!" The room filled with laughter. Cut! Point well taken.

Last night, after spending Thanksgiving Day with family, my mother and I groaned over TV news clips that anticipated today's shopping binge. Many progressives refuse to participate in the orgy of shopping that accompanies the Christmas season. But what about the appropriations for weaponry that are so hard to eliminate from our personal budgets?

I return in memory to a real life scene that happened not far from the birthplace of Jesus. In April of 2002, Jeff Guntzel and I were part of a small team that had entered the Jenin Camp, in Palestine, during the Israeli Defense Force's "Operation Defensive Shield." We were appalled at the conditions afflicting civilians whose homes had been destroyed. One hundred three-story apartment buildings had been reduced to rubble. We had helped pull a grandmother out of a partially destroyed home and, while IDF snipers were still shooting, we'd managed to get a stretcher from a nearby hospital and then carried her to the emergency room, shouting at the soldiers to put their guns down and let us pass.

Later we approached the ruins of a home with two young college-aged Palestinian women. One of the women spotted some fabric and realized it was her jacket. She began clawing through the debris, loosening the fabric from the mound of wreckage, and became increasingly hysterical. Pulling out the jacket in one piece, she went through the pockets, convulsed with nervous laughter over the absurdity. Her sister spotted the edge of a book. Together they dug frantically, as though racing against time, until they unearthed the older sister's nursing textbook and then managed to free another book, a history of Islamic faith. Looking at Jeff and me, the younger woman screamed, "Under here, four televisions, two computers!" They were people, just like us.

The next day, picking our way over more ruined homes, while very brave Palestinian men and boys, wearing flimsy surgical masks, retrieved corpses from the rubble even as IDF snipers were still shooting, we were approached by three furious mothers who saw us scribbling notes in our spiral pads. "Put this in your notebook," shouted one enraged woman. "It is your country that we hold responsible!" She jabbed my notebook. "Write this! Your country!" Taken aback, I blurted out, "I don't pay my taxes." I was desperate not to be responsible.

Who then is responsible? Of course I'm responsible. I live well in the country that, during the 37-year armed Israeli occupation of Palestine, has given over $100 billion dollars to Israel, mostly for its military. U.S. lawmakers have directed the productivity of U.S. people into a $524 billion budget for U.S. military and security in 2005. When I return to the U.S. after spending a few weeks or months in a war-torn, shattered area of the world, how long does it take for me to adjust to electricity, clean water, phones, computers, plenty of food and easy transport? About eight seconds.

There's no way to run or hide from the truth of the U.S. people's responsibility for reckless warfare, military and economic, in numerous parts of the world. Nor can we hide from the truth about who pays to prepare for future wars. In next year's defense budget, $177 billion is earmarked for weapon systems that won't be available until two generations from now. President Bush and his advisors ask that we saddle ourselves, our children and our grandchildren with the bills for this wild spending so that his profiteering friends can become wealthy peddling weapons and war.

Over and over, President Bush told Senator Kerry, "You can run, but you can't hide." It's a harsh line, a hurtful taunt, but in these harsh and hurtful times, the progressive community faces a moral imperative that won't allow us to run or hide. We can't control the U.S. government. Millions of U.S. people tried mightily during the past election season to assert an antiwar agenda. But antiwar progressives can't dodge the fact that more than half of the U.S. democrats voted for Kerry over Dean. More than half the democrats voted for a man who said he would be tougher than Bush on Iraq, but that he'd pursue the war-making more efficiently. He'd have sent more troops than Bush is sending.

Politically, progressives were defeated by a majority of Democrat voters even before the majority of American voters ratified imperialism. We're having limited results from time-honored ways of influencing our government—getting out and protesting, the signs, the candles, the education and legislative work that is still crucially important.

Bush promised that he would spend money for the amount of troops that he needs to recruit for ongoing wars. Most of us are not targeted by the recruiters. We're not listened to by our government, nor, in sufficient numbers, the American people. From most of us, what is required is not our bodies and not our consent—it's our money. This is what we have power over.

We can appropriate money away from militarism to health care, housing and other needs by our resistance, by our nonpayment of taxes for war. As civilian and military casualties mount, as U.S. foreign policy creates terrorists faster than we can kill them, progressives opposed to war-making simply can't deny a moral imperative: don't turn your productivity over to the war-makers.

Our refusal here in the U.S. can be undertaken at no great risk. We're not talking Germany 1939. More relevantly, we're not talking El Salvador 1980-present. By any measure that takes in the lives of our war-victims and the risks they face, it is no great risk.

How readily we criticize Bush for being in denial about the reality of U.S. war-making against Iraq. Yet we're all vulnerable to layers of denial about our own complicity.

In that role-playing scenario, both characters' pleas, both of the mother concerned for her kids and the father concerned for other people's children, were the pleas that persist in Iraq, Afghanistan, the West Bank, impoverished U.S. neighborhoods ("the refugee camps of the class wars," said Dorothy Day), and other war zones. Yearn for peace. Try very hard not to pay for war. And, most of all, think of the children.

Looking The Other Way
December 3, 2004

Shortly before sunrise this morning, a small band of us gathered at a busy Chicago intersection and unfurled vinyl banners bearing enlarged pictures of Iraqi children. One banner called for an end to U.S. warfare in Iraq.

On my banner was Johan, smiling wanly, a fourteen-year-old child who weighed seventy-five pounds shortly before she died of cancer in the oncology ward of a Baghdad hospital on September 21, 2003.

As our banners flapped in the wind, I tried to compose a letter in my head to her teenage brother, Laith, who recently wrote to tell me how much he misses her.

Had Johan lived in a country that wasn't reeling from thirteen years of economic sanctions, she might have survived childhood leukemia. She is one of hundreds of thousands of children who died while economic sanctions and war shattered Iraq's health care delivery system.

Writing my mental letter, I thought of the Rev. Dr. Martin Luther King's words of comfort to bereaved parents of the little girls who were murdered when the Birmingham Baptist church was bombed on September 18, 1963. A former member of the Ku Klux Klan was convicted of the crime. Addie, Carol, Cynthia, and Carole had been praying inside the church.

"These children—unoffending, innocent, and beautiful—were the victims of one of the most vicious and tragic crimes ever perpetrated against humanity," Dr. King said. But he offered comfort. "In a real sense," he continued, "they have something to say to each of us in their death.... They did not die in vain.... Indeed, this tragic event may cause the white South to come to terms with its conscience."

This morning, columnists in major U.S. papers will continue alerting U.S. people to possible wrongs, even crimes, committed by U.N. officials in the course of the Oil- for-Food program which coordinated and monitored sales of Iraqi oil, while economic sanctions ravaged Iraq. Children who committed no crime were brutally—and lethally—punished by sanctions. You aren't likely to find this story in the current exposes of U.N. wrongdoing.

In fact, some U.N. officials tried valiantly to put an end to the economic sanctions. Hans von Sponeck and Denis Halliday resigned their posts and crisscrossed the globe educating people about the effects of the economic sanctions which Halliday termed "genocidal." UNICEF's Executive Director, Carole Bellamy, held a 1999 press conference to announce the release of a "Situation Analysis of Women and Children in Iraq," which carefully explained that the economic sanctions contributed to the "excess deaths" of over 500,000 Iraqi children under age five. Not one U.S. television network aired coverage of the press conference. Only two of fifty leading U.S. papers reported the actual shocking number of one-half million "excess deaths" of children. The *Wall Street Journal* asserted that it was all Saddam's fault. The *New York Times* echoed this in an 800-word story quoting Jamie Rubin of the State Department disparaging the study's methodology.

The sanctions punished children while Saddam's regime profited through smuggling: Many Westerners who traveled to Iraq tried to communicate this to people in their home locales. The smuggling and the illegal rake-offs were no secret, especially in the final years of the sanctions when there were many reports of lucrative kickbacks and inflated prices. Many witnessed the sanctions actually strengthening Hussein's control, as the regime became the only source of food and stability for an increasingly desperate and dis-empowered population.

The children were punished. When the pictures of those little ones—writhing in pain, wrinkled with wasting, desperate and bewildered, held by equally despairing and tortured parents—when those pictures were held up—sometimes as we fasted, sometimes while we were being led off in plastic handcuffs, sometimes at press conferences in front of the U.N. in Baghdad, sometimes in the middle of

Basra cesspools and cemeteries—when those pictures were held up, many people simply looked the other way.

When I try to understand why columnists in far-away places wouldn't take on the story of these worthy victims, I try to remember that there are many worthy victims and one person can't undertake care and concern for every devastating, brutal injustice. Pick your battles. But I can't for the life of me understand how a steady stream of columns have appeared on op-ed pages, in the *New York Times* and other papers, alerting us to possible crimes committed by U.N. officials in the course of the Oil-for-Food program while there has been no mention of the crime of child sacrifice through sanctions and war in Iraq.

The concern currently generating reams of verbiage is that U.N. officials may have looked the other way as Saddam Hussein and a number of collaborators pocketed illegal rake-offs in underhanded dealings using profits from Iraqi oil sales. I'm not equipped to comment on those charges. But is there no columnist who will remind us that 500,000 children under age five died as the U.S. used the U.N. to wage economic warfare against children?

Let's consider the U.N. workers who stood a chance of getting food and medicine into Iraq, were they to look Iraqi families straight in the eyes and say, "Sorry, we'll have to prevent these contracts from going through because you, in your pitiful weakness, can't prevent the dictator who rules you from getting illegal rake-offs on the deal. We can't compromise our principles...."

They looked the other way. I looked the other way myself. In our delegations to Iraq we looked the other way even as we knew that normally we'd be hopping mad and demonstrating in front of any government bastion that inflicted so much fear on its people. But that would have been the end of our access into neighborhoods, families, hospitals, schools. It was a trade-off.

Dr King said, "And so I stand here to say this afternoon to all assembled here that in spite of the darkness of this hour, we must not despair. We must not become bitter.... Somehow we must believe that the most misguided among them can learn to respect the dignity and the worth of all human personality."

But this said, what words of comfort can I offer to Johan's brother Laith? I can tell him where we stood this morning, and whose picture I held. People looked.

Burying Water
December 10, 2004

In the summer of 1994, I was part of a four-person Christian Peacemaker Team dedicated to filing reports on human rights conditions in Jeremie, located in the southern finger of Haiti. When I arrived, I spent one day in Port au Prince, waiting to travel by ferry to the tiny coastal town of St. Helene. That day, eager to be Helpful Hannah, I joined some young girls to haul Hinckley Schmidt-size water containers, destined for a neighborhood center in Port au Prince's appalling Cite Soleil, across a ravine. My arms were trembling almost immediately. When we reached the cement ledge where the plastic water containers were lined up for vehicle transport, I dropped mine down with an exhausted hurrah and then watched in horror as it split. The girls flew into action trying to save some of the precious water. *"Se ou cache verite, ou enterre dlo."* The Haitian proverb says that to hide the truth is like trying to bury water. The truth was gushing out. Throughout that summer I watched women carry water, on their heads, walking miles uphill. One day my friend Madame Ti Pa nearly fainted from the ordeal.

Madame Ti Pa struggled to support three children: Natasha, 8, Petiarson, 2, and Patricia, 1. Natasha was an orphan whose parents were killed when the overcrowded *Neptune* ship capsized off Haiti's coastline. Madame Ti Pa found Natasha wandering tearfully in the street and took her into her home. Natasha was eligible for financial help to attend school, but Madame Ti Pa couldn't afford to buy her a uniform, socks and shoes. Nor did she have money to feed the children properly. The children appeared malnourished and were often feverish. Even so, they sang, laughed and cuddled together, obviously responsive to Madame Ti Pa's animated spontaneity.

St. Helene's hilly roads were rocky and jagged, rough on wheels, shoes, and bare feet. Beyond St. Helene, one path led to a smooth, paved road with attractive interlocking stones called "adoken." Lined by gorgeous plants, trees and flowers, the road passed through the richest section of Jeremie.

Our Christian Peacemaker Team members hurried along this route two mornings each week to make radio contact with Port-au-Prince. The sisters at the House of the Good Shepherd let us use their equipment. Afterward, it was always pleasant to chat with the kindly sisters and to hear of progress at the cooperative farm they sponsored. Sixty-five families were supported by women who cultivated crops in fields next to the sisters' home.

One day, Madame Ti Pa asked me to go with her to talk to the sisters about joining the project. A woman in Port-au-Prince had written her a letter of recommendation. Madame Ti Pa's eyes shone with hope when she showed me the typed letter. Then, she asked for a bar of soap. She hadn't been able to wash clothes for weeks, soap having become a luxury.

Letter in hand, dressed in a clean skirt and top, Madame Ti Pa met me to walk up to the Good Shepherd House. When we reached the smooth road, Madame Ti Pa told me the story behind it. The "adoken" bricks were ordered by President Jean-Bertrand Aristide to build a road through St. Helene, but the shipment was delayed and didn't arrive until after the coup d'etat. The bricks were then confiscated and used instead to cover the already paved road through the richest section of town. The people of St. Helene felt disappointed and cheated.

More disappointment was in store for Madame Ti Pa when we arrived at the Good Shepherd House. Sister Angeline firmly told her that it was impossible for them to accept any more women into the project. Madame Ti Pa was one of many who had begged to join.

Walking back along the "adoken" road, Madame Ti Pa trembled with weakness. She hadn't eaten since the previous morning. I thought again of the attitude I'd heard macoutes express: "The poor are too lazy and stupid to run the country. They just want to cheat and steal." On that road, even the very stones would cry out. (Habakkuk 2: 9-11)

What could we say to people who had driven Haitians to raw despair? Days later I met a man reputed to have committed the worst crimes. He was accused of theft, torture, and murder, yet because he had a gun, he had power. He used this power against simple people who had nothing and craved little more than basic rights. Did I come from a country that had more in common with him or with the people he persecuted?

A shiver ran through me when I recalled similar awareness of the power of water, the power of guns and the crushing weight of poverty encountered in Basra, Iraq during the summer of 2000. Our small peace team of four wanted to settle into the poorest area of Iraq's southern port city to study Arabic and better understand conditions in a neighborhood blighted by the effects of economic sanctions and a dictatorship's abusive rule. Three of the first words I wanted to learn in Arabic were, "Don't do that!" I wanted to shout the phrase at playful boys who, in the blasting heat, would cup their hands, dip into the sewage ditch running alongside the road, and pour filthy water over their heads to cool off. By the end of the summer, my companions and I would sometimes clap our hands over our eyes and shout, "OK, my turn," then pucker our lips as the boys poured water over our heads. The alternative was to pass out under the harsh sun as the temperature rose to 140 degrees.

Each morning, in the household where I stayed, Nadra, whose name means "exceptional," would rise at 4:00 a.m. to begin scrubbing every surface in the sparsely furnished home. Her next task would involve removing a cap stone, lowering an electric pump into the well below, and siphoning off some of the available tap water supply. Nadra was one of a very few people who could afford such a pump. Our team members didn't drink the pumped water, for fear of becoming deathly ill. We drank bottled water and spent more money on two days of bottled water for ourselves than Nadra's household spent for an entire month. So you can see the pecking order: Americans get purified bottled water, an Iraqi family in the good graces of the regime could at least manage to pump somewhat sanitized water, and the poor would be the most vulnerable to water-borne diseases.

Again, memory takes me to a scene of painful conflict over water. I'm remembering a time when our friend Caoihme Butterly walked into the wretched remains of the Jenin Camp on the West Bank, in April of 2002, carrying two heavy six packs of bottled water. Small boys ran up to her, eager to greet her. "Caoihme, Caoihme!" they shouted. Caoihme is a tall woman. She towered over them, holding the valuable water. I watched her eyes fill with tears when the boys, in frustration, began to fight with each other as they reached up to grab her cargo, eager to bring a bottle home to their family.

I wonder how Natasha, the eight-year-old orphan whom I met in St. Helene, has fared. Is she an eighteen-year-old woman with luminous eyes and a gorgeous smile? Would she remember waiting outside her home, each morning, to run and greet me when I stepped out of mine? I hope she doesn't remember a morning when she was crouched on the ground and looked away when I called her name. I walked toward her, wondering if I had done something to hurt the child's feelings the previous day. Drawing closer, I could see tiny pebbles glistening on Natasha's lip. Natasha hadn't run to see me because Natasha was eating dirt.

"You can't bury water," said our Haitian friends. "And you can't bury truth." The British medical journal, *The Lancet*, estimates that upwards of 100,000 Iraqi civilians have died as a result of the war. Child malnutrition is escalating and chronic outbreaks of such diseases as hepatitis and cholera occur regularly.

After 18 months of U.S. war and occupation, contaminated wells cause water-borne diseases. The Tigris and the Euphrates are so polluted that not even animals can safely drink. The lack of electricity means food and medicine can't be preserved and water and sewage can't be treated. Because of chaos and corruption in the U.S. occupation, Iraqis remain in desperate need of jobs, services, and security.

A decade has passed since I first met children in Haiti. Next month, Voices in the Wilderness will mark a decade since we first declared our intent to become "criminals" by traveling to Iraq. Several of our members are returning from recent trips to Haiti with stories worse than mine. I hope the children we've met and all those who hunger and thirst for justice will teach us to tell the truth, nonviolently, and to never be so foolish as to think you can get anywhere by burying water. Many of the people in Haiti and Iraq have the truth but don't have the water. We possess the water, but we lack the truth.

Compiled by Heidi Holliday

Voices in the Wilderness, 1996-2002
A Brief History

December 1995 — Small group of people meet in Chicago and start VitW. The basic idea was to use nonviolent civil disobedience to provoke a confrontation with the powers behind the sanctions against Iraq, which we perceived to be illegal and immoral.

January 15, 1996 — Voices in the Wilderness notified U.S. Attorney General Janet Reno of their intention to deliberately violate the U.S./U.N. sanctions against the people of Iraq by soliciting and transporting medical supplies to Iraq.

January 16, 1996 — Twenty-five people gathered at rally in front of the White House holding up medical supplies and announcing they would deliver them in Iraq. Rallies were also held in Rock Island and Chicago, IL and Birmingham, AL. Seven VitW members arrested at rally in front of White House for refusing to leave the spot the rally was held.

January 22, 1996 — VitW received their first letter from the Office of Foreign Assets Control warning VitW to refrain from engaging in any unauthorized transactions related to the exportation of medical supplies and travel to Iraq.

March 17, 1996 — First Voices in the Wilderness delegation to Iraq.

January 10, 1997 — VitW members held up pictures of suffering Iraqi children during Madeleine Albright's senate confirmation hearings for her appointment as U.S. Secretary of State. Five Voices members were detained and later released. Recognition for Voices in the Wilderness Efforts in 1998: Pax Christi U.S.A Teacher of Peace Award, Newberry Library Free Speech Award.

January 3, 1998 — U.S. Customs detained Kathy Kelly and impounded her passport upon return from a VitW delegation to Iraq. She was issued a new passport in 2000, however, her old one was kept as evidence that she had traveled to Iraq.

January 15, 1998 — Four members of a VitW delegation to Iraq stage a three-day fast outside the United Nations building in Baghdad. VitW members in at least 25 other cities fast or demonstrate to call for an immediate lifting of the sanctions.

February 9–26, 1998 — The 11th delegation of VitW traveled to Iraq at the height of a threatened U.S. attack against Iraq over alleged non-cooperation with weapons inspections. The nine-member delegation was the 1st joint U.S./UK delegation and led to the beginning of VitW-UK

July 25–August 13, 1998, Fast for Life — Voices in the Wilderness members, in repentance for the loss of life caused by the sanctions, gathered in New York City to undertake a vigil and fast, calling for an immediate end to the sanctions. Fasters held a vigil each day and evening at a site opposite the U.S. Mission to the U.N. from July 25, 1998 until U.N. Weapons Inspection Director Richard Butler and Iraq's Deputy Prime Minister Tariq Aziz concluded their round of meetings which was scheduled to begin on August 9, 1998.

September 19–28, 1998 — A group of Voices in the Wilderness members gathered in Duluth, MN for a ten-day, water-only fast. The first eight days of the fast were dedicated to commemorating the eight years of suffering the Iraqi civilians have had to endure since the imposition of the sanctions in 1990. During the last two days, they came together in the hope of a future beyond the cruel sanctions.

November 10, 1998 — As the U.S. again threatened military strikes against Iraq, five Voices in the Wilderness members who traveled to Iraq held a press conference at the Federal Building. Members who returned from Iraq as recently as November 2, 1998 reported on their interviews with U.N. officials in Iraq and the effect of eight years of sanctions imposed on Iraqi civilians. Joined by supporters, members of the group risked arrest in a nonviolent effort to communicate that Iraqi civilians endure lethal use of force every day as a result of U.S./U.N. economic warfare against Iraq.

December 2, 1998 — Voices in the Wilderness received a Pre-penalty Notice from the Department of the Treasury in Washington DC. The notice included Proposed Penalties directed at Voices and four individual delegates: Bert Sacks, Randall Mullins, Dan Handelman, and Joe Zito. Voices was charged with violating the embargo on Iraq through "exportation of donated goods, including medical supplies and toys, to Iraq." The proposed penalty for Voices is $120,000. The proposed penalty for the individual delegates ranges from $10,000-$12,000.

December 17, 1998 — As the U.S. launched military strikes against Iraq, Voices in the Wilderness announced that its 19th delegation left for Iraq. The delegation delivered medicine and medical supplies for children's' hospitals in Iraq in public defiance of U.S. / U.N. sanctions.

Recognition for Voices in the Wilderness Efforts in 1999 — Peace Abbey Courage of Conscience Award. Consortium on Peace Research and Development Social Courage Award. Dan Berrigan Award, De Paul University.

January 15, 1999, Walk Against War — On Martin Luther King's birthday and the eve of the eighth year since the 1991 Gulf War began, Voices in the Wilderness members began an 18-day walk from the Pentagon to the United Nations. Their itinerary included gatherings in Baltimore, Edgewood and Aberdeen, MD, in Wilmington, DE, Chester, PA, Philadelphia, PA, Trenton, Princeton and New Brunswick, NJ and in New York City. Walkers urged the United Nations to "walk away" from war, to no longer allow U.S. foreign policy to pervert the U.N. into being an instrument of warfare against Iraqi civilians. At the U.N., walkers delivered hundreds of signed declarations from people across the U.S. who state that they have deliberately violated the sanctions by contributing toward delivery of medicines to Iraq or by personally traveling to Iraq with medicines and supplies.

February 12-14, 1999 — We Remember, We Resist: A Gathering to End the Economic Sanctions Against Iraq. National Action in New York City and vigils and action nationwide. Organized by VitW, the Fellowship of Reconciliation, and the Atlantic Life Community.

February 17, 1999-April 2, 1999 — Lenten witness to end the U.S. war against Iraq — a national call for fasting, prayer, and action by VitW. During Lent through Good Friday, people wishing to join the Lenten Witness were invited to fast in repentance for the death and suffering the U.S. has inflicted on the Iraqi people. People were encouraged to fast each Friday and more if they felt so moved. Art Laffin conducted a 20-day liquid only fast. Fasters were also invited to pray for a personal and national conversion of heart, away from killing and war-making, to nonviolence and peacemaking and act to end the economic sanctions and the U.S. war against Iraq.

March 1999 Awards — Robert O. Cooper Fellowship in Peace and Justice Award, Southern Methodist University. University of the Incarnate Word Distinguished Speaker Award.

March 4-12, 1999 — VitW members Rick McDowell, Kathy Kelly, and Mike Bremer assisted with a delegation to Iraq organized by the Fellowship of Reconciliation consisting of Nobel Peace Laureates Mairead Maguire (Ireland) and Adolfo Perez Esquivel (Argentina).

June 8-18, 1999 — "Commence with Compassion" Fast and Vigil: Madeleine Albright was to receive an honorary doctorate of law and deliver the commencement address at Northwestern University on June 18, 1999. Six members of the Commence with Compassion fast and vigil began day 8 of the fast by going to Northwestern University President Henry Bienen's office on Tuesday morning, June 15. The Voices in the Wilderness members referred to previous correspondence sent to the President's office expressing their concern over awarding an honorary doctorate of law to Ms. Albright, given her active support of a foreign policy that has violated international law and directly caused the deaths of over 1.5 million Iraqi civilians. The six were later arrested.

August 1999 — Five U.S. congressional aides travel to Iraq with VitW. The delegation was the highest profile delegation from the U.S. to go to Iraq and a great opportunity, not only in raising awareness about the effects of sanctions on Iraq but even more importantly on the legislative side. The delegation's primary focus was the impact of U.S.-U.N. economic sanctions on the humanitarian situation facing Iraqi civilians; they also wanted to examine the question of depleted uranium's continuing effects, and the impact of sanctions on U.S. exports, especially grain, to Iraq, including potential exports post-sanctions.

November 1999 Awards/Recognitions — Office of the Americas Peace and Justice Award. California State Assembly Certificate of Recognition for Founding of Voices in the Wilderness.

November 10, 1999 — Aiming to draw attention to civilian suffering in Iraq, five activists were arrested at the Hilton and Towers Hotel on charges of trespassing during Madeleine Albright's November 10th address to the Chicago Council on Foreign Relations. Those arrested were VitW members Kathy Kelly, Karl Meyer, Danny Muller, Brad Simpson, Kristin Sundell. Fifteen stood to question Ms. Albright on the current suffering in Iraq, while displaying enlarged photos of sick and dying Iraqi children.

Recognition for Voices in the Wilderness Efforts in 2000 — International Fellowship of Reconciliation Pfeiffer Peace Award

January 15-February 14, 2000 — Fasting for Peace With Iraq — End Economic Sanctions — Let Iraq Live. Beginning January 15, 2000, a core group of Voices in the Wilderness members began a month-long fast in Washington DC, intended to end at a retreat gathering in New York City February 12-14, calling for an end to the economic sanctions against Iraq.

February 18, 2000 — VitW/FOR demonstration at the U.S. Mission to the United Nations. Between 250-300 attended the demonstration and 86 were arrested, with reporters from *Time*, CNN, AP, Fox, ABC, and UPI on hand to cover the events. Many reports of the protest piggy-backed news that the top U.N. official in Iraq, Hans von Sponeck, decided to resign. Mr. von Sponeck is the second Humanitarian Coordinator in Iraq to resign in protest of the sanctions (Denis Halliday was the first). Jutta Burghardt, the head of the U.N.'s World Food Program in Iraq, also resigned her post in protest.

April 28, 2000 — The American Friends Service Committee (AFSC) nominated Denis Halliday and Kathy Kelly for a joint 2000 Nobel Peace Prize. "The commitment and courage of these nominees illustrate the far-reaching impact of the actions of individuals in the cause of peace."

June 29, 2000 — VitW members Danny Muller attends an interview with presidential candidate Al Gore and asks, "Mr. Gore, why should anyone vote for an administration that kills five thousand innocent children a month through sanctions in Iraq?" He was removed after Gore refused to answer his question directly.

July 6, 2000 — An activist seeking to end the U.S./U.N. sanctions on Iraq declared victory as he reached a settlement agreement with the U.S. government regarding the return of informational materials seized by Customs in 1997 after he traveled to Iraq. As part of the agreement, the U.S. agreed to pay Dan Handelman of Portland $15,000 in lawyers' fees and damages, as well as returning all the materials seized including film and videotape. Handelman went to Iraq with three other members of Voices in the Wilderness to deliver medicine to children's hospitals.

July 12–September 12, 2000, Six-member VitW peace team completes two-month sojourn to Basra in solidarity with the Iraqi people — The purpose of the delegation was to witness, record, and partake in the experience of living daily life under the ten-year old embargo. Delegation members lived with Iraqi families, without air conditioning or telephones, and subsisted only on the contents of the Iraqi food basket. They also filed weekly reports detailing their activities to various contacts in the United States. Voices members have since used their experiences to further focus attention on the blighted conditions of ordinary Iraqis under the sanctions. On August 6, Voices in the Wilderness held a three-day fast and vigil across from the U.N. headquarters in Baghdad. With activists in Washington, DC and London, they commemorated those killed in Hiroshima and Nagasaki and called for an end to economic sanctions against Iraq. Their statement invited U.N. workers to join them for part or all of the vigil.

National Mobilization to End the Sanctions Against Iraq, Days of Action in DC, August 6–7, 2000 — Marking the tenth anniversary of sanctions, activists from around the country converged on Washington for workshops, training and a march and rally on August 6th. VitW was one of the major organizers.

September 18, 2000 — VitW members visited with Oprah Winfrey's audience before the show and then were able to pose questions to George W. Bush before being escorted out.

October 7, 2000 — Peace activists traveled on the "Omran Bus" from Los Angeles to Vancouver, BC and later around the U.S. to defy U.S. policy and collect school supplies for the children of Iraq. Named for a 13-year-old shepherd killed in May 2000 by the illegal U.S. bombing of Iraq, the Omran Bus Tour was sponsored by Voices in the Wilderness and Middle East Children's Alliance, two groups that have been at the forefront of the struggle to lift the economic embargo on the people of Iraq.

November 11, 2000, Veterans Day 2000 — A national day of protest, prayer, and action to help end the 10-year long sanctions on the people of Iraq. VitW members participate in Day of Silence demonstration commemorating the Iraqi people who have lost their lives because of sanctions.

January 13, 2001, "U.S. to Baghdad Airlift" defies Iraq Sanctions — Twenty-eight religious and humanitarian leaders bound for Baghdad, Iraq, converged on the *U.S.S Intrepid* to challenge the U.S.-led U.N. sanctions on Iraq. They were met there by the "Remembering Omran" Bus, a 40 ft. decorated school bus which has just completed a trans-continental tour sponsored by VitW to educate Americans about the effects of the ongoing U.S.-UK bombing of Iraq. Six members of the group were arrested and cited for criminal trespass after they approached the Museum entrance in order to invite Museum workers to join them in a simple meal.

January 16, 2001 — Ten years since the start of the Gulf War: VitW activists from all over the U.S. held a meal symbolizing effects of the war on the civilian population of Iraq, outside of the U.S. Mission to the U.N. The group shared a simple meal based on the daily food ration of ordinary Iraqi families under the U.N./U.S. economic sanctions against Iraq. The meal consisted of lentils and rice. Unpurified water from the East River was brought to the meal to symbolize the contaminated water that many Iraqis have to drink, because the country has not been allowed the means to restore its water purification systems, destroyed during the Gulf War. After sharing this simple meal, the group attempted to proceed to the U.S. Mission to the United Nations in order to invite Ambassador Richard Holbrook and other workers at the Mission to share the meal and reflect on the deadly effect of U.N. sanctions on Iraqi children and other civilians. Sixteen people were arrested on the steps of the U.S. Mission to the U.N. as they protested ongoing sanctions and bombings of the Iraqi people.

Spring 2001 — Kathy Kelly of VitW was nominated for the Nobel Peace Prize for the second time.

April 7, 2001 — Church members, peace activists and other Iowans who believe the Iowa National Guard's participation in the continued bombing of Iraq is illegal and immoral protested and engaged in a nonviolent blockade at noon at the headquarters of the Iowa Air National Guard in Des Moines.

April 18, 2001, U.S. Citizens Challenge U.N. Resolution on Iraq — Voices in the Wilderness urged members of the U.N. General Assembly not to become immune to the glaring violations of fundamental human rights to education, potable water, and a decent livelihood in a letter to the U.N. Human Rights Commission.

May 31, 2001 — Sign-on Letter for faith-based, humanitarian and human rights organizations to President Bush. Faith-based communities, sponsored by Voices in the Wilderness, delivered a letter to President Bush urging an immediate end to economic sanctions on Iraq.

June 18-27, 2001 — Voices in the Wilderness, led a fast and vigil for the Iraqi people at Federal Plaza in Chicago from June 18 to June 27.

June 21, 2001 — The VitW delegation in Iraq traveled to Mosul and Tel A'fer intent on interviewing survivors of the bombing, relatives of victims, and witnesses. A soccer field at Tel A'fer was bombed at 11:30 a.m. on Tuesday, June 19. The VitW team arrived at noon on Thursday, June 21. They were continuing our five-year effort to communicate the stories and experiences of ordinary people in Iraq as they endure the effects of sanctions and bombardment.

August 6–September 14, 2001, Breaking Ranks — A Fast to End the Siege of Iraq. Besides fasting, participants held daily vigils and leafleted across the street from the U.N. in New York City (the corner of 45th Street and First Avenue), performed street theater, attended Arabic lessons, and held nightly public discussions on the effects of the sanctions. They also sought meetings with U.N. and U.S. representatives. In early September, VitW, in conjunction with local activists across the U.S., organized "Life Under Siege" tent encampments in numerous communities and on college campuses.

August 15, 2001 — Nine participants in the VitW Breaking Ranks fast along with three supporters were arrested for bringing a meal of cooked lentils and rice to the steps of the U.S. Mission to the U.N. Staff members were invited to share the meal and engage in dialogue about how sanctions affect Iraqi civilians. The NYPD jailed the nine for 8–10 hours of "processing."

August 22, 2001 — Ten members of VitW were arrested after bringing a symbolic meal of lentils and rice to the steps of the U.S. Mission to the U.N., inviting members of the staff and the Ambassador's office to share the meal across from the U.S. Mission to the U.N., (45th Street and First Avenue).

September 4, 2001 — Seven VitW members were arrested as they carried a simple meal of cooked lentils and rice to the steps of the U.S. Mission to the U.N., having invited staff members to share the meal and talk with them about why they are on their 30th day of a fast to end the sanctions against Iraq. Three previous efforts to share a meal and initiate conversation met with arrest and charges of trespass and obstruction.

September 11, 2001 — VitW members fasting in New York City agree to end their public presence and complete the remaining week of the fast in prayerful silence. Two days later, U.S. Mission to the U.N. workers invited the fasters to a meeting.

November 25–December 3, 2001, A Walk for Healing and Peace — Washington, D.C. to New York City. Family members of 9/11 victims led the peace walk, saying "Our Grief is Not a Cry For War." Voices in the Wilderness, in cooperation with numerous other organizations, endorsed the walk, and several Voices members joined in the walk.

December 27, 2001 — Several members of the forty-first Voices in the Wilderness delegation to Iraq brought new blood bags from the United States as a gift to one of Iraq's hospitals and then donated their own blood for use in the hospital's ward serving children with leukemia.

January 14, 2002 — Iraq Activists Offer Hugs, Cookies, and Counseling to "Battered" U.N. A group of American peace activists and Iraqi street children held a demonstration at U.N. Headquarters in Baghdad, offering U.N. workers milk and cookies, as well as free hugs and counseling. The group, from Voices in the Wilderness, likened the U.N. to a "battered woman in need of help," and the U.S. to "her abuser."

January 22, 2002 — People from across the U.S. gathered in front of the U.S. Mission to the U.N., advocating a change in U.S. foreign policy that would continue the legacy of peacemaking begun by Dr. Martin Luther King, Jr. In the spirit of King's anti-war stance, 55 men and women occupied the steps of the mission, demanding an end to the war in Afghanistan and renouncing any possible expansion of the war. The act of nonviolent civil disobedience was the culmination of a four-day series of presentations and training reflecting on the life of Dr. King.

April 7, 2002 — Kathy Kelly and Jeff Guntzel left Chicago for Israel/Palestine, along with three Catholic Worker companions. They remained in the region until April 25. Each felt very compelled by the extraordinary witness of Palestinians, Israelis and internationals who, at considerable risk, have nonviolently resisted the Occupation, invasion and acts of random violence that afflict people in Israel and Palestine. They returned from the Jenin camp with ample evidence that the Israeli government ordered Israeli Occupying Forces to commit crimes against humanity by attacking and destroying a civilian neighborhood in the Jenin refugee camp.

May 24-30, 2002, Compassion Iraq Coalition Peace Walk to Baghdad — VitW members organized "Walk for Peace" across Iraq Desert. The sanctions-defying walk raised funds for cancer-stricken Iraqi children. Sixteen Americans journeyed to Iraq to participate in the seven day walk across the desert to dramatize the need for the U.S. and the international community to "go the extra mile" in averting the all-out war against that country reportedly being planned by the Bush administration.

June 17, 2002, Declaration 2002 — Press conference to announce Bert Sacks' noncompliance with the $10,000 fine imposed on him by OFAC for bringing medicine and food into Iraq. He instead raised $10,000 for medicine to be sent to Iraq.

August 3–September 11, 2002 — Voices in the Wilderness sponsored a second 40-day fast entitled "Break Ranks — Build Bridges" in New York City across the street from the U.S. Mission to the U.N. Fasters encouraged the member states of the U.N. to "break ranks" with the U.S. in its insistence on endless sanctions for Iraq as well as to oppose any new U.S.-led military onslaught against Iraq.

September 12, 2002 — Voices in the Wilderness joined Pax Christi New York and other concerned groups to begin the "Mirror of Truth" Bus Tour on a three-month trip visiting weapons sites and speaking all along the East Coast, ending at the gates of the School of the Americas during SOA Watch's annual vigil and protest in Ft. Benning, GA in November.

In October 2003 — the first members of the Iraq Peace Team, a project of the VitW campaign, took up residence in Iraq. Iraq Peace Team members remained in Iraq throughout the Shock and Awe bombing and the first year of the U.S. led occupation.

Continued history of VitW campaign efforts can be found at their website: www.vitw.org

Suggestions for using portions of this book in peace studies coursework will be posted at the Voices in the Wilderness website. For more information, contact Voices at: 1460 West Carmen Avenue, Chicago, IL 60640, 773-784-8065 info@vitw.org

Afterword from the Publishers

KATHY KELLY STANDS FOR MEMORY. THROUGH THE JUBILANT DECADE of the 1990s, with Bill Clinton at the helm of Empire, Kelly and her companions at Voices in the Wilderness made regular trips into the darkness of Iraq, bearing witness to the world that the Gulf War of 1991 had not ended but had merely entered a terrible, though partially hidden (to those with no zeal to see) new phase, where sanctions became the weapon of choice and civilians the intended target.

The sanctions against Iraq, imposed by the U.N. at the behest of the U.S., barred the shipment of medical equipment, medicines, food, and even toys. The weight fell most viciously on the old, the poor, the infirm and, especially, children. By the U.N.'s own count, more than 500,000 children perished as a direct result of the sanction regime—child sacrifices in the ongoing war against Saddam.

Kathy Kelly and her fellows ventured to Iraq dozens of times over those years bearing gifts: medical supplies, food, toys for children. The world press corps had largely decamped to cover the dot.com economy, the Simpson trial, the Lewinsky affair. Kelly's journals and letters from those extended visits in Iraq, collected in **Other Lands Have Dreams,** provides a vivid and unique history of how Iraq was subjected to a kind of long-distance torture by the U.S. and its indentured servant, the U.N. Her book is a living history, written through the eyes of Iraqi mothers, children, students, doctors and musicians, whose lives have been overturned by more than a decade of war and deprivation, inflicted in the name of humanitarianism.

While the global press was infatuated with smart bombs and cruise missiles, Kelly writes hauntingly of the aftermath of the war: about having to live without electrical power, about hospitals without basic equipment to sustain the lives of sick patients, about streets overflowing with raw sewage because the treatment plants bombed during the Gulf War couldn't be rebuilt under the merciless grip of the sanctions.

This is a history of the U.S. war on Iraq that never appeared in the pages of the New York Times or in the news stories on CNN. Her visits did not go unnoticed by U.S. authorities. The State Department, under the command of Madeleine Albright, who infamously told Leslie Stahl that the child deaths caused by the sanctions "were worth it", sent threatening letters. The Treasury Department, through its Office of Foreign Assets, hit Kelly and her colleagues at Voices in the Wilderness with $20,000 fines for breaching the sanctions and bringing medicine to sick children.

Bush justified his invasion of Iraq on fraudulent allegations of Iraq's stockpile of Weapons of Mass Destruction and support for international terrorism. At home, Kathy Kelly lead protests against the U.S.'s stockpiles of nuclear weapons and training school for exporting terrorism through Latin America, the School of the Americas at Fort Benning, Georgia. Her non-violent protests at nuclear sites in Missouri and Wisconsin landed her in federal prisons. So did her demonstration outside the gates of the School of the Americas, which trained the torturers and assassins that killed and maimed thousands across El Salvador, Honduras and Colombia.

Last year, when we looked back on the reports Kathy Kelly had sent us from Iraq and which had won her and her group a huge following on our CounterPunch website we could think of no book we would be prouder to publish in CounterPunch Books than a collection of her reports from Iraq, from Haiti and from two U.S. prisons. Kathy Kelly stands in the tradition of Dorothy Day, of the Berrigans and those other courageous souls who have added such luster to the annals of the Catholic Worker movement. The literature of resistance is what inspires the next generation to go forth and battle for the good and the true. Here is a book which offers that inspiration in full measure.

Jeffrey St. Clair
Alexander Cockburn

Index

AK Press

ORDERING INFORMATION

AK Press
674-A 23rd Street
Oakland, CA 94612-1163
U.S.A
(510) 208-1700
www.akpress.org
akpress@akpress.org

AK Press
PO Box 12766
Edinburgh, EH8 9YE
Scotland
(0131) 555-5165
www.akuk.com
ak@akedin.demon.uk

The addresses above would be delighted to provide you with the latest complete AK catalog, featuring several thousand books, pamphlets, zines, audio products, video products, and stylish apparel published & distributed by AK Press. Alternatively, check out our websites for the complete catalog, latest news and updates, events, and secure ordering.

Also Available from AK Press

The first audio collection from Alexander Cockburn on compact disc.

Beating the Devil

Alexander Cockburn, ISBN: 1 902593 49 9 • CD • $14.98

In this collection of recent talks, maverick commentator Alexander Cockburn defiles subjects ranging from Colombia to the American presidency to the Missile Defense System. Whether he's skewering the fallacies of the war on drugs or illuminating the dark crevices of secret government, his erudite and extemporaneous style warms the hearts of even the stodgiest cynics of the left.

Next from CounterPunch/AK Press

COMING FALL/WINTER, 2005

The Case Against Israel by Michael Neumann

Wielding a buzzsaw of logic, Professor Neumann dismantles plank-by-plank the Zionist rationale for Israel as religious state entitled to trample upon the basic human rights of non-Jews. Along the way, Neumann also offers a passionate amicus brief for the plight of the Palestinian people.

Also Available from CounterPunch and AK Press,
(call 1-800-840-3683 or order online at www.akpress.org)

Dime's Worth of Difference: Beyond the Lesser of Two Evils
Edited by Alexander Cockburn and Jeffrey St. Clair

Everything you wanted to know about one-party rule in America.

Whiteout: the CIA, Drugs and the Press
by Alexander Cockburn and Jeffrey St. Clair, VERSO.

The involvement of the CIA with drug traffickers is a story that has slouched into the limelight every decade or so since the creation of the Agency. In Whiteout, here at last is the full saga.

Been Brown So Long It Looked Like Green to Me: the Politics of Nature
by Jeffrey St. Clair, COMMON COURAGE PRESS.

Covering everything from toxics to electric power plays, St. Clair draws a savage profile of how money and power determine the state of our environment, gives a vivid account of where the environment stands today and what to do about it.

The Golden Age Is In Us
by Alexander Cockburn, VERSO.

Cockburn's classic diary of the late 80s and early 90s. *"A Patchwork Paradise Lost"*, *Times Literary Supplement*. *"A literary gem"*, *Village Voice*.

Imperial Crusades: Iraq, Afghanistan and Yugoslavia
by Alexander Cockburn and Jeffrey St. Clair, VERSO.

A chronicle of the lies that are now returning each and every day to haunt the deceivers in Washington and London, the secret agendas and the underreported carnage of these wars. We were right and they were wrong, and this book proves the case. Never leave home without it.

Why We Publish CounterPunch
By Alexander Cockburn and Jeffrey St. Clair

Ten years ago we felt unhappy about the state of radical journalism. It didn't have much edge. It didn't have many facts. It was politically timid. It was dull. CounterPunch was founded. We wanted it to be the best muckraking newsletter in the country. We wanted it to take aim at the consensus of received wisdom about what can and cannot be reported. We wanted to give our readers a political roadmap they could trust.

A decade later we stand firm on these same beliefs and hopes. We think we've restored honor to muckraking journalism in the tradition of our favorite radical pamphleteers: Edward Abbey, Peter Maurin and Ammon Hennacy, Appeal to Reason, Jacques René Hébert, Tom Paine and John Lilburne.

Every two weeks CounterPunch gives you jaw-dropping exposés on: Congress and lobbyists; the environment; labor; the National Security State.

"CounterPunch kicks through the floorboards of lies and gets to the foundation of what is really going on in this country", says Michael Ratner, attorney at the Center for Constitutional Rights. "At our house, we fight over who gets to read CounterPunch first. Each issue is like spring after a cold, dark winter."

YOU CANNOT MISS ANOTHER ISSUE

The Politics of Anti-Semitism

Edited by Alexander Cockburn and Jeffrey St. Clair

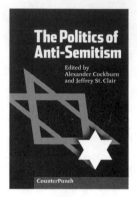

What constitutes genuine anti-Semitism—Jew-hatred—as opposed to disingenuous, specious charges of "anti-Semitism" hurled at realistic, rational appraisals of the state of Israel's political, military and social conduct?

There's no more explosive topic in American public life today than the issue of Israel, its treatment of Palestinians and its influence on American politics.

Yet the topic is one that is so hedged with anxiety, fury and fear, that honest discussion is often impossible.

The Politics of Anti-Semitism lifts this embargo.

Powerful Essays By

Michael Neumann	Scott Handleman
Alexander Cockburn	Lenni Brenner
Uri Avnery	Linda Belanger
Bruce Jackson	Robert Fisk
Kurt Nimmo	Will Youmans
M. Shahid Alam	Norman Finkelstein
Jeffrey St. Clair	Jeffrey Blankfort
George Sunderland	Kathleen and Bill Christison
Yigal Bronner	Edward Said

Reviews

"Michael Neumann's essay, "What Is Anti-Semitism," by and of itself is worth forking over the $12.95 to get a copy of *The Politics of Anti-Semitism*. ...There is much more in *The Politics of Anti-Semitism* that deserves attention. ... But, of particular note are the essay of Yigal Bronner, a member of Ta'ayush, the Arab-Jewish Partnership, and professor at Tel Aviv University, and one of the last essays of Edward Said, before he lost his life to cancer. Both of them offer a sane and humane vision in which Israelis and Palestinians are able to live together, side by side, with all their diversity and commonality, in peace. They conclude the collection fittingly, with hope for the future."

Gilles d'Aymery: www.swans.com

"This is a superlative discussion, with important lessons for all. Many of the essays in this book have appeared on the CounterPunch website—an important online magazine which is edited by the editors of this book. Cockburn, St. Clair and the other authors must be commended for addressing this important topic with this collection of excellent essays. Unfortunately, criticism of Israel is still a taboo topic, and the first ones to raise questions will probably attract a significant amount of abuse. One must remember this when appreciating the courage of those who have produced this important book."

Paul de Rooij: Washington Report on Middle East Affairs

Available from CounterPunch and AK Press
(call 1-800-840-3683 or order online at www.akpress.org)

Other Titles from AK Press

Books

MARTHA ACKELSBERG – *Free Women of Spain*

KATHY ACKER – *Pussycat Fever*

MICHAEL ALBERT – *Moving Forward: Program for a Participatory Economy*

JOEL ANDREAS – *Addicted to War: Why the U.S. Can't Kick Militarism*

PAUL AVRICH – *The Modern School Movement: Anarchism and Education in the United States*

ALEXANDER BERKMAN – *What is Anarchism?*

ALEXANDER BERKMAN – *The Blast: The Complete Collection*

HAKIM BEY – *Immediatism*

JANET BIEHL & PETER STAUDENMAIER – *Ecofascism: Lessons From The German Experience*

BIOTIC BAKING BRIGADE – *Pie Any Means Necessary: The Biotic Baking Brigade Cookbook*

JACK BLACK – *You Can't Win*

MURRAY BOOKCHIN – *Anarchism, Marxism, and the Future of the Left*

MURRAY BOOKCHIN – *Ecolgy of Freedom*

MURRAY BOOKCHIN – *Post-Scarcity Anarchism*

MURRAY BOOKCHIN – *Social Anarchism or Lifestyle Anarchism: An Unbridgeable Chasm*

MURRAY BOOKCHIN – *Spanish Anarchists: The Heroic Years 1868–1936, The*

MURRAY BOOKCHIN – *To Remember Spain: The Anarchist and Syndicalist Revolution of 1936*

MURRAY BOOKCHIN – *Which Way for the Ecology Movement?*

MAURICE BRINTON – *For Workers' Power*

DANNY BURNS – *Poll Tax Rebellion*

MATT CALLAHAN – *The Trouble With Music*

CHRIS CARLSSON – *Critical Mass: Bicycling's Defiant Celebration*

JAMES CARR–*Bad*

NOAM CHOMSKY – *At War With Asia*

NOAM CHOMSKY – *Language and Politics*

NOAM CHOMSKY – *Radical Priorities*

WARD CHURCHILL – *On the Justice of Roosting Chickens: Reflections on the Consequences of U.S. Imperial Arrogance and Criminality*

HARRY CLEAVER – *Reading Capital Politically*

ALEXANDER COCKBURN & JEFFREY ST. CLAIR (ed.) – *Dime's Worth of Difference*

ALEXANDER COCKBURN & JEFFREY ST. CLAIR (ed.) – *Politics of Anti-Semitism, The*

ALEXANDER COCKBURN & JEFFREY ST. CLAIR (ed.) – *Serpents in the Garden*

DANIEL & GABRIEL COHN-BENDIT – *Obsolete Communism: The Left-Wing Alternative*

EG SMITH COLLECTIVE – *Animal Ingredients A–Z (3rd edition)*

VOLTAIRINE de CLEYRE – *Voltarine de Cleyre Reader*

HOWARD EHRLICH – *Reinventing Anarchy, Again*

SIMON FORD – *Realization and Suppression of the Situationist International: An Annotated Bibliography 1972–1992*

YVES FREMION & VOLNY – *Orgasms of History: 3000 Years of Spontaneous Revolt*

DANIEL GUERIN – *No Gods No Masters*

AGUSTIN GUILLAMON – *Friends Of Durruti Group, 1937–1939, The*

ANN HANSEN – *Direct Action: Memoirs Of An Urban Guerilla*

WILLIAM HERRICK – *Jumping the Line: The Adventures and Misadventures of an American Radical*

FRED HO – *Legacy to Liberation: Politics & Culture of Revolutionary Asian/Pacific America*

STEWART HOME – *Assault on Culture*

STEWART HOME – *Neoism, Plagiarism & Praxis*

STEWART HOME – *Neoist Manifestos / The Art Strike Papers*

STEWART HOME – *No Pity*

STEWART HOME – *Red London*

STEWART HOME – *What Is Situationism? A Reader*

KATHY KELLY – *Other Lands Have Dreams: From Baghdad to Pekin Prison*

JAMES KELMAN – *Some Recent Attacks: Essays Cultural And Political*

KEN KNABB – *Complete Cinematic Works of Guy Debord*

KATYA KOMISARUK – *Beat the Heat: How to Handle Encounters With Law Enforcement*

RICARDO FLORES MAGON – *Dreams of Freedom: A Ricardo Flores Magon Reader*

NESTOR MAKHNO – *Struggle Against The State & Other Essays, The*

G.A. MATIASZ – *End Time*

CHERIE MATRIX – *Tales From the Clit*

ALBERT MELTZER – *Anarchism: Arguments For & Against*

ALBERT MELTZER – *I Couldn't Paint Golden Angels*

RAY MURPHY – *Siege Of Gresham*

NORMAN NAWROCKI – *Rebel Moon*

HENRY NORMAL – *Map of Heaven, A*

HENRY NORMAL – *Dream Ticket*

HENRY NORMAL – *Fifteenth of February*

HENRY NORMAL – *Third Person*

FIONBARRA O'DOCHARTAIGH – *Ulster's White Negroes: From Civil Rights To Insurrection*

DAN O'MAHONY – *Four Letter World*

CRAIG O'HARA – *Philosophy Of Punk, The*

ANTON PANNEKOEK – *Workers' Councils*

BEN **REITMAN** – *Sister of the Road: the Autobiography of Boxcar Bertha*

PENNY **RIMBAUD** – *Diamond Signature, The*

PENNY **RIMBAUD** – *Shibboleth: My Revolting Life*

RUDOLF **ROCKER** – *Anarcho-Syndicalism*

RON **SAKOLSKY** & STEPHEN **DUNIFER** – *Seizing the Airwaves: A Free Radio Handbook*

ROY **SAN FILIPPO** – *New World In Our Hearts: 8 Years of Writings from the Love and Rage Revolutionary Anarchist Federation, A*

ALEXANDRE **SKIRDA** – *Facing the Enemy: A History Of Anarchist Organisation From Proudhon To May 1968*

ALEXANDRE **SKIRDA** – *Nestor Makhno – Anarchy's Cossack*

VALERIE **SOLANAS** – *Scum Manifesto*

CJ **STONE** – *Housing Benefit Hill & Other Places*

ANTONIO **TELLEZ** – *Sabate: Guerilla Extraordinary*

MICHAEL **TOBIAS** *Rage and Reason*

TOM **VAGUE** – *Anarchy in the UK: The Angry Brigade*

TOM **VAGUE** – *Great British Mistake, The*

TOM **VAGUE** – *Televisionaries*

JAN **VALTIN** – *Out of the Night*

RAOUL **VANEIGEM** – *Cavalier History Of Surrealism, A*

FRANCOIS EUGENE **VIDOCQ** – *Memoirs of Vidocq: Master of Crime*

GEE **VOUCHER** – *Crass Art And Other Pre-Postmodern Monsters*

MARK J **WHITE** – *Idol Killing, An*

JOHN **YATES** – *Controlled Flight Into Terrain*

JOHN **YATES** – *September Commando*

BENJAMIN **ZEPHANIAH** – *Little Book of Vegan Poems*

BENJAMIN **ZEPHANIAH** – *School's Out*

HELLO – *2/15: The Day The World Said NO To War*

DARK STAR COLLECTIVE – *Beneath the Paving Stones: Situationists and the Beach, May 68*

DARK STAR COLLECTIVE – *Quiet Rumours. An Anarcha-Feminist Reader*

ANONYMOUS – *Test Card F*

CLASS WAR FEDERATION – *Unfinished Business: The Politics of Class War*

CDs

THE **EX** – *1936: The Spanish Revolution*

MUMIA **ABU JAMAL** – *175 Progress Drive*

MUMIA **ABU JAMAL** – *All Things Censored Vol.1*

MUMIA **ABU JAMAL** – *Spoken Word*

FREEDOM ARCHIVES – *Chile: Promise of Freedom*

FREEDOM ARCHIVES – *Prisons on Fire: George Jackson, Attica & Black Liberation*

JUDI **BARI** – *Who Bombed Judi Bari?*

JELLO **BIAFRA** – *Become the Media*

JELLO **BIAFRA** – *Beyond The Valley of the Gift Police*

JELLO **BIAFRA** – *High Priest of Harmful*

JELLO **BIAFRA** – *I Blow Minds For A Living*

JELLO **BIAFRA** – *If Evolution Is Outlawed*

JELLO **BIAFRA** – *Machine Gun In The Clown's Hand*

JELLO **BIAFRA** – *No More Cocoons*

NOAM **CHOMSKY** – *American Addiction, An*

NOAM **CHOMSKY** – *Case Studies in Hypocrisy*

NOAM **CHOMSKY** – *Emerging Framework of World Power*

NOAM **CHOMSKY** – *Free Market Fantasies*

NOAM **CHOMSKY** – *New War On Terrorism: Fact And Fiction*

NOAM **CHOMSKY** – *Propaganda and Control of the Public Mind*

NOAM **CHOMSKY** – *Prospects for Democracy*

NOAM **CHOMSKY/CHUMBAWAMBA** – *For A Free Humanity: For Anarchy*

WARD **CHURCHILL** – *Doing Time: The Politics of Imprisonment*

WARD **CHURCHILL** – *In A Pig's Eye: Reflections on the Police State, Repression, and Native America*

WARD **CHURCHILL** – *Life in Occupied America*

WARD **CHURCHILL** – *Pacifism and Pathology in the American Left*

ALEXANDER **COCKBURN** – *Beating the Devil: The Incendiary Rants of Alexander Cockburn*

ANGELA **DAVIS** – *Prison Industrial Complex, The*

JAMES **KELMAN** – *Seven Stories*

TOM **LEONARD** – *Nora's Place and Other Poems 1965–99*

CASEY **NEILL** – *Memory Against Forgetting*

CHRISTIAN **PARENTI** – *Taking Liberties: Policing, Prisons and Surveillance in an Age of Crisis*

UTAH **PHILLIPS** – *I've Got To know*

DAVID **ROVICS** – *Behind the Barricades: Best of David Rovics*

ARUNDHATI **ROY** – *Come September*

VARIOUS – *Better Read Than Dead*

VARIOUS – *Less Rock, More Talk*

VARIOUS – *Mob Action Against the State: Collected Speeches from the Bay Area Anarchist Bookfair*

VARIOUS – *Monkeywrenching the New World Order*

VARIOUS – *Return of the Read Menace*

HOWARD **ZINN** – *Artists In A Time of War*

HOWARD **ZINN** – *Heroes and Martyrs: Emma Goldman, Sacco & Vanzetti, and the Revolutionary Struggle*

HOWARD **ZINN** – *People's History of the United States: A Lecture at Reed College, A*

HOWARD **ZINN** – *People's History Project*

HOWARD **ZINN**–*Stories Hollywood Never Tells*

DVDs

NOAM **CHOMSKY** – *Distorted Morality*

ARUNDHATI **ROY** – *Instant Mix Imperial Democracy*